THE
MARTIN
HARRIS
STORY

with biographies of
Emer Harris and Dennison Lott Harris

by
Madge Harris Tuckett
and
Belle Harris Wilson

Illustrations by Rich Holdaway

THE MARTIN HARRIS STORY
(Insert)

This Volume is an exact reprinting of the 1983 first edition of *The Martin Harris Story* by Madge Harris Tuckett and Belle Harris Wilson. It could be rated as a "classic collectors edition," and will surely be a valuable addition to any library. The co-authors are qualified research genealogists and retired school teachers now eighty-six and ninety years of age respectively. They spent ten years researching material for this book. The sisters descend from Emer Harris, an older brother and frequent missionary companion to Martin Harris.

The reader will be fascinated by Martin's determination, sacrifice and faith. Here was an abundantly talented, prominent man who lost his home, his 150-acre form and eventually his family by following the Lord's command to aid in the first printing of the *Book of Mormon.*

Efforts to reprint this current edition were inspired by a talk given by Elder Dallin H. Oaks of the Quorum of the Twelve, a great-great grandson of Emer Harris. Elder Oak's mother, the late Stella H. Oaks, was a sister to the co-authors. In the April 1999 General Conference of the Church of Jesus Christ of Latter-day Saints Elder Oaks said, "Having a special interest in Martin Harris, I have been saddened at how he is remembered by most church members. He deserves better than to be remembered solely as the man who unrighteously obtained and then lost the initial manuscript pages of the *Book of Mormon....* We obviously honor Joseph for his magnificent ministry, but Martin's subsequent faithfulness continues under a shadow from which this important man should be rescued."

The co-authors are grateful to Ned Warner for printing the original edition and this current volume. The original edition has been out of print for some time. This edition was produced by cutting apart an original copy of *The Martin Harris Story* to make printing plates. The result is an exact copy of the original book at an affordable price.

Erratum

The first edition of *The Martin Harris Story* was published in 1983. On page 24, the first three lines are a reference to documents dealer Mark Hofmann and the Anthon transcript. Hofmann admitted in 1987 that he had forged the purported Anthon transcript as well as other documents. Hofmann was convicted of two murders relating to the sale of other fraudulent documents and was sentenced to life in prison.

FOREWORD

Sufficient rhetoric has been published about Martin Harris, the Book of Mormon witness, and ample has been assumed and accepted, but not enough has been published about Martin Harris, the Man.

"The evil that men do lives after them; the good is often interred with their bones."—Shakespeare. This writing includes statements of Martin Harris' weaknesses, but we wish to repudiate the on-going impressions that he was ever formally tried for his membership or ever departed from the witness given him of the reality of the Book of Mormon plates or the divinity of their message.

We two sisters, descendants of Emer Harris (brother to Martin Harris, witness to the Book of Mormon) have spent many years of research and more than one year putting together what we feel is a fair and accurate account of the life of Martin Harris.

Ever since our youth we have heard and read opinions set forth as truth in church publications which are not supported by fact. This book is well documented and filled with factual information, most of which has never before been published or presented in its true light.

No writer in one hundred and fifty years has presented any new views on his life. To us this was a virgin field. We know by personal experience that most people are not well informed on the life of this divinely appointed man. This experience gave opportunity to collect much accurate and worthwhile information.

We feel that no one person contributed more financial support to the church in its infancy than did Martin Harris, and yet few have been chastened as he, with his weaknesses published to the world (Doctrine and Covenants).

One must realize, also, that the period in which his weaknesses were paramount offered a time when he could—but did not—deny the witness of the reality of the plates on which the Book of Mormon was written, or the divinity of their message.

We hope the reader is *eager* to know more of the man who contributed so significantly at crucial times in church history.

PREFACE

On assembling the material which now comprises an accurate account of Martin Harris, we (the authors) should not deny the directives from the spirit which have become so meaningful to us. These have not come as overwhelming numbers of related facts but as knowledge of the sources from which information could be obtained. At times we have been awakened and overcome with the directives we have received. We also have been brought to our knees in response to our needs to have others see this man as he really was.

Young Joseph Smith depended on Martin's diplomacy and good judgment as he sent him to Columbia College to meet with the distinguished linguists of that day. Lucy Mack Smith furnished a proper example in her diary when the translation of the plates was finally completed: "We conveyed this intelligence to Martin Harris, for we loved the man although his weakness had caused us much trouble."

We the authors have felt a great love for him as the total events of his life have unfolded. His great heart saw the temporal needs of the young prophet and responded with his means without any desire for repayment.

The active opposition from Martin's own wife, Lucy, could not turn him from his avowed financial support for the publication of the Book of Mormon. In spite of this his great heart entertained no animosity toward her and he made verbal statements of his love for her.

Who among us today would give up wife, children, a prestigious home and considerable property in order to further the work of this church?

Martin Harris was given the responsibility by the prophet of securing a publisher for the forthcoming Book of Mormon. This was accomplished only through considerable effort.

Citizens of the early community of Palmyra, New York, considered him an honest and upright citizen and a kind and benevolent neighbor. His industry is attested to by the recognition he received from the Ontario Agricultural Society as well as in the property which he acquired by his own industry and efforts. He should now be recognized for the great qualities which he did possess.

The Lord who knows the beginning from the end, no doubt reserved a place for Martin Harris with the stalwarts recognized among the founders of the church. We along with hundreds of others are proud to be his kinsmen and look forward to associating with him during the eternities.

DEDICATION

*To those who have believed
in the inherent goodness and integrity
of Martin Harris.*

CONTENTS

TO THE MEMORY OF
MARTIN HARRIS

Witness thou wert and art,
  Through grace divine
Of holy records, what a boon was thine.
  Honored beyond most mortals
By the Lord
  To be a special witness of His word.

Down through the ages shall thy
  Honored name in holy writ
Its truth divine proclaim
  One of the Three permitted to
Behold those holy records
  Writ on plates of gold.

"Though dead yet Speaketh"
  Can be said of thee,
O, thou beloved, while resting here thou be.
  Far o'er the world this message
Now is heard.
  A witness faithful to his holy word.

Rest thou in peace;
  Thy testimony true, by millions
Shall be sought to read and view.
  View and behold and full
Salvation win, who find
  The path that thou did enter in.

Words by Evan Stephens
Era, May 1937, Volume 30
L.D.S. Song Book, old edition

Chapter I

Background of Greatness

Wintergreen Hill in Palmyra, New York, is a proud hill. Not that it is of any great importance in and of itself, but past events have given it a rightful claim to prominence. It has been the back-drop for the stage of events that have now changed the beliefs of millions of people. In days long past, it was a favorite spot for native hunters of deer, elk, and bear. Wild apple trees blossomed and bore fruit on its slopes. Some may be aware that in days long past a look-out was posted upon its highest knoll to ensure that no unannounced war party of Indians could arrive to wipe out the fledgling settlement. Such an attack had nearly been accomplished once, but this would not happen again. Later, the plant from which the hill derives its name became so abundant on its slopes that the leaves were harvested and marketed throughout the land as a flavor delight.

None of this, however, is the cause for present-day fame. That fame has come from sacrifice alone, in the sur-render of 150 acres of its farmland and an elaborate home constructed, not only of the finest materials available, but of dreams of future happiness and prosperity. These were sacrificed when Martin Harris committed his means to pay for the publication of the ancient sacred record, *The Book of Mormon*.

To understand this event we must know something of the heritage of this man and some of the experiences that marked him for such a calling.

Martin's fore-bears were courageous men and women who craved religious freedom and for that reason left England's shores in 1630 with Roger Williams to face unknown hardships in Rhode Island. When Williams became a "seeker," the Harrises soon followed. Martin's parents, Nathan and Rhoda Lapham Harris, showed the same cour-age by leaving the flourishing area of that early colony to move to upstate New York, first to Cambridge, Washington County, where their eldest son, Emer, was born on May 29,

3

1781. Martin was born May 18, 1783, in Easton, Saratoga, New York. Seven additional children were born to them, the last one in Palmyra, New York.

The five older children appear with these parents in the 1790 census of Washington County, New York State. No additional information is available on this family or their life in that area, or how long they were located there. It is known, however, that they were among the first settlers who in 1793 were induced by John Swift to settle the undeveloped region of western New York. Swift had purchased considerable land from Phelps and Gorham Company for the purpose of resale and had persuaded adventuresome settlers from the states of Massachusetts, Connecticut, and Rhode Island to move to that area. Among them were relatives of both Nathan and his wife. Rufus Harris, a brother from Smithfield, Rhode Island, came early with his family. He was the father of Peter Harris, a Quaker minister, and nine other children. Also arriving early were Abraham, Benjamin, and David Lapham, residents of Adams, Massachusetts, and Aretas Lapham, a native of Burrillville, Rhode Island.

Nathan Harris and his wife had responded to an inner drive that can only be explained by the roles their sons were destined to play. On February 3, 1794, Nathan purchased 600 acres, which was nearly a square mile of property in this new undeveloped section called Swifts Landing. (This area is now known as Palmyra, having also been called Canal Town.) For this land he paid three or four shillings an acre. Such an amount of cash suggests that his motive in relocating was not lack of success at those former settlements.

Nathan and Rhoda were among the first settlers, and their resourcefulness and industry are equaled by only a few of their contemporaries. Although but nine years of age, Martin was to be involved in the strenuous activities of pioneer life. The land was heavily timbered. It needed to be cleared, the wood sawed into lengths suitable for home use and piled. This implies a never-ending job of filling the wood box. Martin would also have been a mother's helper in procuring for drying the abundant fruits and berries. Emer, his older brother, helped their father plant crops between the numerous stumps. Cattle were herded endlessly, since they must not wander over the cultivated land or go too far astray. Cows had to be milked twice daily. Domestic animals were continually coveted by the roving Indians and had to be watched closely. Sometimes the boys would capture a small rodent for a pet, but often its cunning put an end to their plans. One may conjure a picture of this small family in the firelight of their log shelter talking of the day's work and news of their former associates, news eagerly received from the oncoming settlers.

The drive Nathan and Rhoda must have had for instilling in their offspring the rudiments of proper learning must not be overlooked. Harris names are not found on the rolls of Palmyra's earliest schools, but the experiences and accomplishments of their later lives proclaim the ability to read with understanding, cipher with accuracy, write legibly and convincingly, and reason clearly.

Of necessity, each household aimed to be self-sufficient. Each settler had his own tannery and shoe shop where he prepared the leather to make and mend shoes. Parents carded their own wool, spun their own rolls, and wove their own yardage into cloth or knitted yarn into needed articles. They dipped their own candles, made their own soap, sewed and wove their own rage carpets.

"Nathan, Martin's father, according to an account in the *Palmyra Courier*, built his log house at the north end of Wintergreen Hill, then barren of timber . . . cleared a small spot of ground, planted some fruit trees and as the settlement progressed, became more and more a sportsman."[1]

Nathan Harris is listed as being present at the first town meeting, April 1796, at the Gideon Durfee home, where he was elected path master when paths of buffalo, moose, and elk were only tentative routes through the deep vegetation of a land where year-round precipitation is the standard. The office of path master was not considered an easy one, as only a trail led to Nathan's log cabin and to those of the other settlers. A Mr. Thomas L. Cook records these traditions:

It is interesting to read reminiscences of Palmyra's pioneer settlers, many of whom had thrilling experiences with the Indians, predatory animals, etc. Bears would frequently carry off hogs and calves alive, and even break into smoke-houses and take hams and bacon. Wolves would raid the sheep and poultry flocks and play havoc with them. The villagers had declared war on these night prowlers and had reduced their numbers to near zero; but there was one big timber wolf that defied the villagers in their efforts to snare him. Once or twice each week he visited the village and carried away some pet goose or slayed one or more sheep. The villagers finally organized a hunting party with the determination to rid the community of this night marauder. [2]

When quite an old man he shot the last wolf killed in this vicinity. This wolf made its appearance in the neighborhood and committed some depredations; a company including Nathan Harris, Stephen Phelps and others, set out to capture him, and as Harris was riding along the road on his old horse, he discovered the wolf crossing the road, and, putting the old horse into a gallop, while loading his gun, got so near that he shot and killed the wolf while his horse was under full headway.

Nathan Harris loved dearly to hunt and fish, to attend "raisings," and could play ball even in his old age, with all the enthusiasm of youth. He knew where all the deep places in the streams were to be found, the summer resorts of the speckled autocrats; their watering places; their Saratogas. He also possessed a sort of marvelous knowledge regarding the exact time when fish would bite the best. His neighbors never went fishing when he stayed at home; they knew from experience that when Uncle Nathan went, then was the time, and he went so often there was no need of going between times. He was as much of a hunter as a fisher and was known as the Nimrod of this settlement.

Beyond the house on the west side of the road was a spring of clear cold water in which he kept trout, and of one he made a pet, teaching him all that was necessary for a trout to know. This trout not only served as a monitor to tell when the time was propitious for fishing, but gained for him a sobriquet or nickname that followed him through life. In time it got to be a very large trout and well educated so that it would jump at times from the water and seize grasshoppers or other bait which would be held out from time to time.

. . . One day, Nathan Harris had an old friend call to see him . . . who had an unusually large red nose. . . . The two old friends went out to visit the farm and finally came around to the spring. It was a warm day in early summer and the old friend seeing so good an opportunity for a drink, got down on all fours to partake of the cooling effects of nature's beverage. Nathan looked on, and as the big red nose came near the water, out sprang the trout and seized the end of it which caused a sudden and furious jerk of the head landing the trout some ten feet in the rear of the impractical water drinker. So frightened was the friend and so carried away with laughter was Harris by this joke of the trout, that, for a time, neither knew what they were about. This, however, did not last long and Harris, after returning the trout to the spring, assured his friend that it was a most propitious time to go a fishing and that he would treat him to some rare sport; which he did, as they bagged a fine lot of the speckled beauties in the afternoon. If that trout had kept in the bottom of the spring, there would have been no trout taken from Red Creek that day; the old acquaintance would have missed the best of his visit, and Uncle Nathan would not have borne the name of "Trout Harris," a name by which he was ever afterwards universally known.

Nathan Harris Farm, Palmyra, New York

In the spring of the year when wild ducks were plenty, he used to post himself on a bend in the creek, and bring them down with his long fowling piece as they were flying over. In wet weather he had a cover for the lock of his gun, made from the skin of a deer's shank, so dried and fitted as to form a complete cover for the old fashioned flint lock, and when the ducks or pigeons came in sight he would throw back the top part which was hinged to the under part, and drawing a quick sight scarcely ever failed of bringing some of them down. The settlers would often find bullets in trees while chopping and knew them to be his, from the great weight of the ball used in his rifle. It was said that some of the roads, which were quite crooked in his neighborhood, were first laid out as his hunting paths. There were no game laws in his days, and no season of the year but furnished him with his favorite diversions of hunting or fishing. In the latter amusement he was as much of an adept as in the former and as a trout fisher he had no equal.[2]

After living in a log house for some time, Nathan built a new frame house that was still standing (in 1949), looking very much as when first built, except for a north wing added in 1845.[3]

A husking frolic that took place at Nathan's house in 1796 is described by Mrs. Eden Foster, who was in attendance: "We had a pot pie baked in a five pail kettle [10 gallon iron kettle] composed of 13 fowls, as many squirrels, and due proportions of beef, mutton and venison; baked meats, beans and huge pumpkin pies. Hunting stories, singing, dancing on a split basswood floor, *snap and catch 'em, Jumping the broom stick* and *hunt the squirl*, followed the feast. All joined the rustic sports, there was no aristocracy in those days."[4]

Again from the *Palmyra Courier:* "On such occasions [Nathan] was the center figure of the group, and whatever in the way of a joke that was aimed at 'Uncle Nathan' was always received in the best of humor. He was a public man, ready for fun on public occasions but willing that others should accept of public duties as well as public honors."[5]

It may have been at this or another similar gathering where 25-year-old Martin became romatically attracted to 16-year-old Lucy, his cousin, the daughter of Rufus Harris. No doubt she was a vivacious, attractive young woman, though nine years his junior. She was known by her contemporaries as a Quaker, as was her brother, Peter. They were married March 27, 1808, in Palmyra, Ontario County, New York.[6] Martin had obtained 150 acres of land that had previously belonged to his father. The deeds were recorded October 12, 1813.[7] Each of Nathan's sons subsequently received part of his original property, with Martin's extending southward near the banks of the Erie canal and in time numbering 320 acres, most of which he obtained by his own efforts.

The Harrises were hard-working, frugal people. As a result, by 1824 Martin had a prestigious frame home of one and one-half stories, painted white, containing perhaps eight or more rooms. There were barns and sheds across the way, constructed of rough hemlock boards. At this time mud was knee deep in the main streets of Palmyra, and other settlers were yet living in log cabins. The population at that time was nearly twenty-five hundred.

In 1890, Thomas Gregg wrote *The Prophet of Palmyra*. Among other things, he stated that he was yet a boy when Martin and his wife visited the Gregg home. "None in all that neighborhood were more promising in their future prospects than they. . . . [Harris] is declared to be a gentleman and a farmer of respectability." Martin is also described in the *Palmyra Courier*:

> as an industrious, hardworking farmer, shrewd in business calculations, frugal in habits, and what is termed a prosperous man of the world . . . until the summer of 1828. Shortly, previous to this, he had become somewhat religiously awakened and began to study the *Bible*. He also became quite skeptical, as well as superstitious, believing in miracles, wonderful dreams, spiritual interpositions, special provi-

10

dences, etc. He pursued the study of the *Bible* with great tenacity, committing to memory whole books and at the time of the Mormon incubations, could quote chapter and verse with surprising correctness. He bore the reputation in Palmyra of being an honorable and upright man and an obliging and benevolent neighbor.

Early in the life of Martin Harris the Lord had prepared in him a proper foundation for that which was to come. Quoting from a letter dictated in his old age and written "by a borrowed hand" to a religious inquirer, he revealed this early spiritual background:

The Lord showed me there was no true church upon the face of the earth, none built upon the foundation designed by the Savior 'The rock of revelation' as declared to Peter. See Matthew XVI 16, 17, 18 verses. He also showed me that an angel should come and restore the Holy Priesthood again to the earth and commission his servants again with the holy Gospel to preach to them that dwell on the earth: See Revelations XIV 6, 7 verses. He further showed me that the time was nigh when he would 'set His hand again the second time to restore the Kingdom of Israel . . . when He would bring the record of Joseph which was in the hand of Ephraim and join with the record of Judah when the two records become one in the hand of the Lord to accomplish his great work in the last days. See Ez. 36th and 37th chapter to the end of the book also Psalms 50. The Lord has shown me these things by his spirit . . . by administration of holy angels . . . and confirmed the same with signs step by step, as the work has progressed for the space of fifty three years . . . write again and we will endeavor to enlighten you on any point relative to this doctrine.

I am very respectfully

Martin Harris Sr.[8]

(Journal History, Jan. 1, 1877, pp. 1–2)

Lucy and Martin had been married only a few years when the War of 1812 broke out, Martin being twenty-nine years of age. Being a man of means, he could have hired a substitute to fill his own draft duty, as others often did, but he chose to fulfill his own assignment. "Martin served as a private and a teamster in a Battle at Buffalo, New York, in 1813. He was a first sergeant in the 39th New York Militia, commanded by Pardon Durfee under Colonels Howell and Rogers in the Battle of Puttneyville, May 1814. He was mustered out at this same point and later discharged there."[9]

Martin Harris' ambition and versatility cannot be doubted. In addition to the strenuous life of the owner of such a large acreage, he engaged in pursuits that many farmers would later leave to itinerate weavers. These farmers provided a separate shed where workmen would set up proper equipment for the purpose of supplying the family with yardage for its household needs or for those of a bride-to-be.

Each resident furnished wool for this process, and also flax for linens—every farmer in the area being required to raise at least one acre. The European source of flax had been cut off at the time of the American Revolution, and so it had been necessary to establish complete self-sufficiency with that commodity. Flax grew well in this area, as it does anywhere corn will grow. Early weavers used a combination of wool and flax, which accounts for the survival today of treasured pieces of tapestries and coverlets.

Local households needed to manufacture dyes if they wanted color, using local weeds, flowers, and roots. They also performed the tedious, time-consuming task of preparing the materials for weaving.

Women probably did very little of the early weaving. The looms were large; shifting the harnesses, controlling the treadle, and beating in the weft to produce the intricate patterns desired, required a man's strength.

Martin Harris' weaving preceeded the coming of commercial weavers to this locality, his competence should be recognized. The following extractions from local newspapers over a three-year period attest to his tenacity and skill.

12

Quoted from the Ontario Repository, Oct. 29, 1822, from the Ontario Agricultural Society Premiums:

Domestic Manufactures—to Martin Harris, Palmyra, for the best cotton and woollen coverlet, $5.00.

To Martin Harris, Palmyra, for the next best (looks to be about 2nd place) 20 yrds. of bleached linen, 7–8 wide, $4.00.

November 11, 1823:

Martin Harris, Palmyra, for the next best (2nd place) 20 yards of worsted cloth, or Bombazett, for women's wear, $5.00.

Martin Harris, Palmyra, for the next best (2nd place) four pairs of worsted stockings, $3.00.

Martin Harris, Palmyra, for the fourth best 20 yards of flannel, $3.00.

Martin Harris, Palmyra, for the next best (2nd place) pair of rose blankets; $5.00.

Martin, Harris, Palmyra, for the best cotton and woollen coverlet, $5.00.

M. Harris, Palmyra, for the next best (2nd place) cotton and Woollen coverlet, $3.00.

Martin Harris, Palmyra, for the best 20 yards bleached linen cloth, 78 wide, $8.00.

Martin Harris, Palmyra, for the manufacture of bed ticking and coverlets, $2.50.

The *Wayne Sentinel*, November 10, 1824, of Palmyra, New York, noted these awards from the Ontario Agricultural Fair:

Martin Harris of Palmyra for the best pair of rose blankets.

To Martin Harris of Palmyra for the best 20 yards bleached linen, 7–8 wide.

Early Barge on the Erie Canal

When the Erie Canal was completed October 24, 1825, Martin found himself in an enviable position, his land being in close proximity to it. This canal was indeed a benefactor to early-day Palmyra, as it opened up markets that before were almost inaccessible. It became a shipping place to both north and south. Residents saw a steady stream of barges or boats both night and day in the seasons when it was free of ice. In 1825, the year it was completed, 13,110 boats with forty thousand people went by Utica, New York. Arriving in Albany June 15, 1827, were 67 boats, carrying fourteen thousand bushels of wheat and other grain. Thirty-five boats cleared at the same time as well as other crafts making an average of eleven for every daylight hour. Before this time it cost a hundred dollars a ton to ship produce to Albany and New York City, but by barge on the canal it was offered at between nine and ten dollars a ton. [10] All Martin's surplus now had a ready market. He shipped livestock and grain to the cities, having the animals slaughtered on arrival and the meat sold from the docks. These circumstances brought unforseen prosperity to a man whom destiny had favored for a specific purpose.

Joseph Smith, Sr., arrived in Palmyra in 1816, and the Smiths and the Harrises became close friends. The Smiths lived first in the village of Palmyra near the town square. In 1824, their association with the Harrises became more intimate when Father Smith and Hyrum were engaged in walling up a basement, laying a foundation, and digging and curbing a well and cistern for Martin. The Smiths confided in Martin the details concerning Joseph Smith's first vision and he intimated his inclination to accept the vision.

> Each day while they were there, Martin would find excuse to bring up the matter and would ask many questions, referring frequently to the Bible to prove that heavenly messengers visiting the earth was not a new doctrine. Finally, during the course of their conversations, Mr. Smith took Martin into his confidence and told him of Joseph's wonderful experi-

ence with the angel, Moroni. Martin was thrilled beyond expression. He requested that he be kept posted on any new developments.[11]

The family was reluctant to discuss it elsewhere, but they made Martin their confidant, relating the circumstances of the angel Moroni's visit to Joseph in the upper room of the Smith's original log house in September, 1823. Their trust was rewarded as their account of that heavenly manifestation found fertile soil in Martin's heart.

Years later Martin said that the Prophet Joseph Smith was very poor and that he often gave Joseph work on his farm. They had frequently hoed corn together, Martin paying him for each day's work. He said Joseph was a good worker and jovial, and they often wrestled together in sport. Martin was told in confidence of the existence of the Book of Mormon plates by Joseph Smith, Sr., two or three years before Joseph obtained them.

Hill Cumorah, Palmyra, New York

Chapter II
Rebuked and Reinstated

What the relationship between Martin Harris and his wife, Lucy, had been before this time cannot be clearly ascertained, but Mother Smith hints at it when she recorded, "Her husband always allowed her to keep a private purse in order to satisfy her singular disposition. . . ."[12]

The rumor of Martin's generosity to the Prophet must have reached Lucy's ears. No doubt in an effort to appease her, he deeded to her eighty acres of land. At that time in this area of New York, there was an old Dominion law then in effect, prohibiting the transfer of property directly to a wife by her husband. Thus, on November 29, 1825, Martin deeded this property first to Peter Harris, Lucy's brother (not Martin's), who the same day redeeded it to Lucy.[13]

According to Cook in *Palmyra and Vicinity*, Peter Harris came to Palmyra, New York, in 1825 and bought the little thirty-acre farm that had once been a part of the Nathan Harris tract. He and his wife, "Aunt Nabbie," as she was called, lived there for many years. In his youth, Peter had been a sailor, but after coming to live on this farm he became a Quaker minister.

On September 22, 1827, Joseph Smith, Jr., received the gold plates from the Angel Moroni. No sooner was it known that he had them, than the most strenuous efforts were used to get them from him. Mother Smith relates:

With the view of commencing the work of translation and carrying it forward as speedily as circumstances would permit, Joseph came to me and requested me to go to Martin Harris and inform him that he [Joseph] had the plates and that he desired to see Mr. Harris concerning the matter. This, indeed, was an errand which I much disliked as Mr. Harris' wife was a very peculiar woman, one that was naturally of a very jealous disposition. Besides this she was rather dull of hearing and when anything was said that she did not hear distinctly, she sus-

17

pected that it was some secret which was designedly kept from her. So I told Joseph that I would rather not go, unless I could have the privilege of speaking to her first upon the subject.[14]

Mother Smith went to the Harris home. She records her impressions:

> She [Lucy] did not wait for me to get through with my story before she commenced urging upon me a considerable amount of money that she had at her command . . . . saying she could spare two hundred dollars.
>
> . . . She considered herself altogether superior to her husband and she continued her importunities. . . .
>
> She also had a sister living with her who desired me to receive an amount of money, I think some seventy-five dollars, to assist in getting the record translated.[15]

The sister mentioned was Lucy's sister, Polly, widow of Freeman Cobb, who was drowned on Lake Ontario December 19, 1821. This is the same Mrs. Cobb to whom Joseph Smith referred in connection with the Book of Mormon manuscript.[16] She and her children lived in the home with Martin and Lucy Harris at Palmyra, New York, until she remarried.

After refusing the money, Mother Smith requested the privilege of speaking to Mr. Harris. Mrs. Harris went with Mother Smith to where Martin was working. He stated that he would not stop work as he was laying the last brick in his hearth.

> "You see," said he, "this is the last work I have to do on the house, and it is the last work I shall do about the house, or on the farm, in one year."
> . . . and when this is done I am going to hire a hand to work a year for me, as I shall travel that length of time before I shall settle myself at home again."
>
> After completing the work in which he was engaged, he left the house but was absent only a short

time. On returning he came to me and said, "Now I am a free man — my hands are altogether untied — I can come and go and do as I please."

. . . I related, in short, the errand on which I had come. He said that he would see Joseph in the course of a few days. At this his wife exclaimed, "Yes, and I am coming to see him, too, and I will be there on Tuesday afternoon and will stop over night."[17]

On their arrival, Lucy Harris spent some time questioning Joseph about the plates. If the plates really existed, she wanted to help publish them. She also demanded to be shown the record. Her demand was, of course, refused.[18] Her statements as recorded by Mother Smith reveal her attitude: "Now Joseph, are you not telling me a lie? Can you look full in my eye and say before God that you have in reality found a Record, as you pretend?"[19]

The Harrises remained that night in the home with the Smiths. When they arose the next morning, Lucy Harris related a remarkable dream that had followed her inappropriate actions of the day before. In the dream,

She [Lucy] said that a personage appeared to her who told her that, as she had disrupted the servant of the Lord, and said his word was not to be believed, and had also asked him many improper questions, she had done that which was not right in the sight of God. After which he [the personage] said to her, "Behold, here are the plates, look upon them and believe."

After giving us an account of her dream, she described the Record very minutely.[20]

Before this incident, Joseph had decided to move to Harmony, (now Oakland) Pennsylvania, to the home of his wife's parents, Mr. and Mrs. Isaac Hale. His brother-in-law, Alva Hale, came to Palmyra in December, 1827, to move Joseph and Emma to Harmony. Mother Smith recorded:

19

He [Alva Hale] and Joseph were one day in Palmyra . . . . transacting some business. As they were thus engaged, Mr. Harris came in: he stepped immediately up to my son and taking him by the hand said, "How do you do, Mr. Smith." After which he took a bag of silver from his pocket and said again, "Here, Mr. Smith, is fifty dollars; I give this to you to do the Lord's work with; no, I give it to the Lord for his own work."[21]

When Joseph suggested that he sign a note for the money, Mr. Harris insisted that he would give the money to the Lord and called those present to witness the fact that he gave it freely and did not demand any compensation. Joseph's wardrobe needed replenishing, and Harris, who was abundantly able to do as he did, procured for him a new black suit, remarking that it was necessary that he should appear comely before men; and consequently ordered the best pattern in the store.[22] Joseph and Emma journeyed to the home of Emma's parents shortly afterward, taking with them the sacred gold plates and arriving there in the month of December.

Joseph had been instructed to make a facsimile of some of the characters, which were called "reformed Egyptian," and send them to some of the most learned men of that generation and ask them for the translation. This should lay aside once and for all the long-accepted notion that Martin made this journey on his own volition and with the attitude of a "doubting Thomas." Martin and Joseph had agreed that when Joseph had had sufficient time to transcribe some of the Egyptian characters, Martin would follow him, and Martin would take the characters to the East to professed linguists to give them an opportunity to translate them.

When Lucy discovered what her husband had in mind, she resolved to accompany him, but Martin left quite suddenly without her knowledge. When Mrs. Harris missed her husband, she went to Mother Smith and accused her of arranging the whole affair.

Martin traveled to Harmony, Pennsylvania where Joseph gave him the copy of characters from the plates with his translation of them.

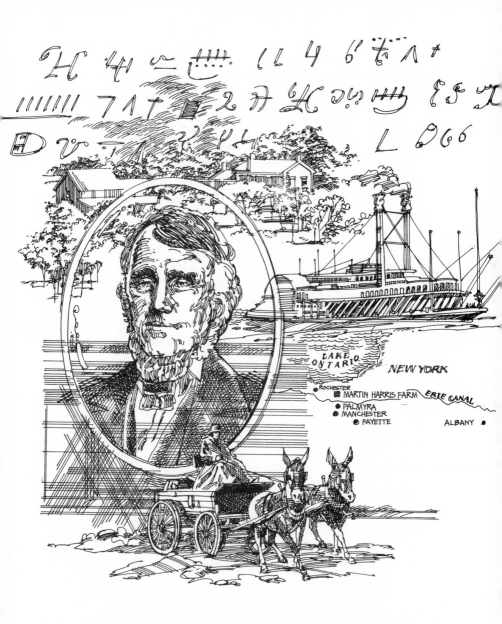

"Martin . . . in a small wagon drawn by a team of
mules in February 1828, traveling alone . . .
      New York City was a distance of between four
hundred and five hundred miles."

The original note was written by Joseph Smith and carried by Martin Harris as he traveled east.[23]

Martin undertook this venture in a small wagon drawn by a team of mules in February, 1828, traveling alone on miles of unimproved roadways. The college to which he went was the forerunner of Columbia University today. New York City was a distance of between four and five hundred miles. Martin was fulfilling the prophecy in Isaiah 29:11-12, which predicts: "And the vision of all is become unto you as the words of a book that is sealed; which men deliver to one that is learned saying, Read this . . . and he saith, I cannot; for it is sealed: And the book is delivered to him that is not learned."

Martin reported his experience to Joseph. Joseph Smith recorded the incident in his *History of the Church* (Vol. I, p. 20) as retold by Martin Harris:

> I went to the city of New York, and presented the characters which had been translated, with the translation thereof, to Professor Charles Anthon, a gentleman celebrated for his literary attainments. Professor Anthon states that the translation was correct, more so than any he had before seen translated from the Egyptian. I then showed him those which were not yet translated, and he said that they were Egyptian, Chaldaic, Assyric, and Arabic; and he said they were true characters. He gave me a certificate, certifying to the people of Palmyra that they were true characters, and that the translation of such of them as had been translated was also correct. I took the certificate and put it into my pocket, and was just leaving the house, when Mr. Anthon called me back, and asked me how the young man found out that there were gold plates in the place where he found them. I answered that an angel of God had revealed it unto him.
>
> He then said to me, "Let me see the certificate." I accordingly took it out of my pocket and gave it to him, when he took it and tore it to pieces, saying, that there was no such thing now as ministering of

angels, and that if I would bring the plates to him, he would translate them. I informed him that part of the plates were sealed, and that I was forbidden to bring them. He replied, "I cannot read a sealed book." I left him and went to Dr. Mitchell, who sanctioned what Professor Anthon had said respecting both the characters and the translation.

Professor Anthon, however, gave a somewhat conflicting story years later. The unpopular position that the Church of Jesus Christ of Latter-day Saints held at that time would account for this; also, the time which had elapsed before Professor Anthon told his story—a matter of "selective memory."

Quoting now from a letter by Martin Harris under a later date of November 23, 1870, he states:

"Mr. Emerson, Sir: I received your favor. In reply I will say concerning the plates, I do say that the angel did show to me the plates containing the Book of Mormon. Further, the translation that I carried to Professor Anthon was copied from the same plates; also, that the professor did certify to it being a correct translation, I do firmly believe and do know that Joseph Smith was a Prophet of God; for without I know he could not have had that gift, neither could he have translated the same. I can give if you require it, one hundred witnesses to the proof of the Book of Mormon. I defy any man to show me any passage of scripture that I am not posted on to the best of my knowledge; if you can rely on my testimony of the same. In conclusion I can say that I arrived in Utah safe, in good health and spirits considering the long journey. I am quite well at present, and have been, generally speaking, since I arrived.

With many respects I remain your humble friend.

MARTIN HARRIS
Smithfield, Utah
(*Millennial Star*, 1 Jan. 1877)

23

The recent findings by Mark Hofmann of the original Book of Mormon characters as copied by Joseph Smith and delivered to these linguists substantiates the above accounts. Joseph Smith wrote: "These characters were dilligently copied by my own hand from the plates of gold and given to Martin Harris who took them to New York City but the learned could not translate it because the Lord would not open it to them in fulfilment of the prophecy of Isaiah written in the 29th chapter and 11th verse."[24]

Martin Harris, having returned from this tour, left Joseph in Harmony, Pennsylvania, and returned home to Palmyra, New York.

When Martin began to make preparations to start for Pennsylvania the second time, to act as scribe for Joseph when translating, Lucy Harris insisted on going along. Joseph's mother wrote:

> As soon as she arrived there, she informed him [Joseph Smith] that her object in coming, was to see the plates, and that she would never leave until she had accomplished it. Accordingly, without delay, she commenced ransacking every nook and corner about the house—chests, trunks, cupboards, etc.; consequently, Joseph was under the necessity of removing both the breast-plate and the Record from the house, and secreting them elsewhere. Not finding them in the house, she concluded that Joseph had buried them, and the next day she commenced searching out of doors, which she continued to do until about two o'clock p.m. She then came in rather ill-natured; after warming herself a little, she asked Joseph's wife if there were snakes in that country in the winter. She [Emma] replied in the negative. Mrs. Harris then said, "I have been walking round in the woods to look at the situation of your place, and as I turned round to come home, a tremendous black snake stuck up his head before me, and commenced hissing at me."

The woman was so perplexed and disappointed in all her undertakings, that she left the house and took lodgings during her stay in Pennsylvania with a near neighbor in Harmony. According to Joseph's mother, "While this woman remained in the neighborhood, she did all that lay in her power to injure Joseph in the estimation of his neighbors."[25]

Later testimony reveals that when Lucy Harris returned home, being about two weeks in Harmony, she endeavored to dissuade her husband, who had driven her home, from taking any further part in the publication of the record. However, Martin Harris paid no mind to her attitude on this matter. Joseph wrote, "Mr. Harris . . . arranged his affairs, and returned again to my house about the 12th of April, 1828, and commenced writing for me while I translated from the plates, which we continued until the 14th of June following, by which time he had 116 pages of the manuscript on foolscap paper."[26]

Before the translation began, Joseph and Martin curtained off the east end of an upstairs room, including a window, and began their work. "Although in the same room, a thick curtain or blanket was suspended between them, and Smith concealed behind the blanket. . . . He looked through his spectacles, or transparent stones, and would write down or repeat, what he saw; which when repeated aloud was written down by Harris who sat on the other side of the suspended blanket. . . . This was Harris's own account to me."[27]

The translation of the ancient characters was made by Joseph Smith, using the Urim and Thummim (called "interpreters"). They are described by Joseph Smith as consisting of two precious stones set in an arch of silver, fastened to an ancient breastplate. As they were focused upon the small and beautifully engraved characters, the translation thereof was revealed.

The gold plates were uniform in thickness, about like common tin, and engraved on both sides. They were bound together by three large rings like a book (See *History of the Church*, Vol. 1, pp. 12-13).

Home of Joseph Smith, Harmony, Pennsylvania, where most of the Book of Mormon was translated.

Even after entering into the work of translation in 1828 as Joseph Smith's first secretary, Martin Harris was vigilant. Upon returning to the Church in 1870 Martin reminisced of these days. The summer translation project was tedious, especially to active men accustomed to physical labor, so they broke the tension by recesses at the nearby Susquehanna River, where they exercised by throwing stones into the water. Finding a stone "very much resembling the one used for translation," Martin made a substitution without Joseph Smith's knowledge. The translator became confused and then frustrated, exclaiming, "Martin! What is the matter?" His scribe's guilty expression revealed the situation to the Prophet, who demanded an explanation. Martin's answer shows how constantly the secretary was on guard against deception: "To stop the mouths of fools, who had told him that the Prophet had learned those sentences and was merely repeating them."[28]

It was at this time, however, that the loss of the manuscript pages occurred, a loss disasterous for both Martin and Joseph. According to Joseph, "Sometime after Mr. Harris began to write for me, he began to importune me to give him liberty to carry the writings home and show them."[29]

William Pilkington, Jr., a lad in the home where Martin Harris spent the last years of his life, sheds some light on this situation as he tells the following: "Martin's wife was opposed to her husband having anything to do with Joseph Smith. She was very bitter against him . . . but if Joseph would let him bring the manuscript home she would like to see it . . . so accordingly he asked the prophet, which he did through the Urim and Thummim, and the answer was 'no'."[30]

Martin, realizing his wife's attitude and determination, asked Joseph to ask the Lord again for permission to take the 116 pages home to show his irate wife, but the answer remained the same.

"Poor Martin was unfortunately gifted with a troublesome wife; her inquisitive and domineering nature made him dread unpleasant results from his present engagement. His manuscript had reached 116 pages, and he there-fore begged permission to read it to her 'with the hope that it might have a salutatory effect upon her feelings.' "[31]

"It is quite certain that neither Joe [Joseph] Smith nor Martin Harris had intelligence nor literary qualifications adequate to the production of a work of this sort. Who then was it's author?"[32]

Emma Smith (Bidamon) gives her long-cherished memories of the translation of the Book of Mormon in the following words when asked the question, "What is your belief about the authenticity or origin of the Book of Mor-mon?": "My belief is that the Book of Mormon is of divine authenticity — I have not the slightest doubt of it. I am satisfied that no man could have dictated the writing of the manuscript unless he was inspired; for, when acting as scribe, [as Emma did for a short time] your father [Joseph Smith, Jr.] would dictate to me hour after hour, and when returning after meals or after interruptions he would at once begin where he left off, without either seeing the manuscript or having any portion of it read to him. This was an unusual thing for him to do. It would have been impos-sible that a learned man could do this; and for one so ignorant and unlearned as he was, it was simply impossi-ble."[33]

When Martin told Lucy he had been denied the privilege of showing her the translation, she became very angry and insisted that he ask a third time. "At this time Martin said she was awful worked up and threatened to kick him out of the house if he didn't bring the manuscript home."

Martin told William Pilkington, "Willie, I loved my wife and wanted to please her. . . . I found out, Willie, that the Lord could get out of patience, as well as a human."[34]

This later account implies that Martin had returned to Palmyra after the translation of the first 116 pages and before he finally secured them. Martin bound himself with an oath to show the 116 pages of manuscript to only these five people: his parents, Nathan and Rhoda Harris; his brother, Preserved; Lucy, his wife; and her sister, Mrs.

Cobb. Many people have given accounts of the "missing manuscript" of which we will quote.

After leaving Joseph, Martin arrived at home with the manuscript in safety. Soon after, he exhibited the manuscript to his wife and family. His wife was so pleased with it, that she gave him the privilege of locking it up in her own set of drawers, which was a special favor, for she had never before this allowed him even the privilege of looking into them. After he had shown the manuscript to those who had a right, according to his oath, to see it, he went with his wife to visit one of her relatives, who lived some ten or fifteen miles distant.

After remaining with them a short time, he returned home, but his wife declined accompanying him back. Soon after his return, a very particular friend of his made him a visit, to whom he related all that he knew concerning the Record. The man's curiosity was much excited, and as might be expected, he earnestly desired to see the manuscript. Martin was so anxious to gratify his friend, that although it was contrary to his obligation, he went to the drawer to get the manuscript, but the key was gone. He sought for it some time, but could not find it. Resolved, however, to carry his purpose into execution, he picked the lock, and, in so doing, considerably injured his wife's bureau. He then took out the manuscript, and after showing it to this friend, he removed it to his own set of drawers, where he could have it at his command. Passing by his oath, he showed it to any good friend that happened to call on him.

When Mrs. Harris returned, and discovered the marred state of her bureau, her irascible temper was excited to the utmost pitch, and an intolerable storm insued, which descended with the greatest violence upon the devoted head of her husband.

Having once made a sacrifice of his conscience, Mr. Harris no longer regarded its scruples; so he continued to exhibit the writings, until a short time before Joseph arrived, to any one whom he regarded as prudent enough to keep the secret, except our family, but we were not allowed to set our eyes upon them.

For a short time previous to Joseph's arrival, Mr. Harris had been otherwise engaged, and thought but little about the manuscript. When Joseph sent for him, he went immediately to the drawer where he had left it, but, behold it was gone! He asked his wife where it was. She solemnly averred that she did not know anything respecting it. He then made a faithful search throughout the house, as before related.

The manuscript has never been found; and there is no doubt but Mrs. Harris took it from the drawer, with the view of retaining it until another translation should be given, then to alter the original translation, for the purpose of showing a discrepancy between them, and thus make the whole appear to be a deception.[35]

We now quote Pomroy Tucker, a contemporary of Martin Harris:

[Martin] was accordingly permitted to take the manuscript translation into his possession. Reading a portion of them to his wife, a Quakeress of positive qualities, she denounced the whole performance as silly and impious. His neighbors and friends, whom he importuned and bored on the subject, uniformly expressed the same sentiment and belief and cautioned him againt being imposed upon and defrauded.

But this opposition served only to strengthen Harris's profession of faith.[36]

We can sympathize with Martin as we remember the opposition he had met on every turn from Lucy for his support of the young Joseph Smith. Lucy had not accepted in any degree the divinity of the work in which her husband was involved. No doubt much had been explained and confided at its onset, but Lucy was not receptive. It is most likely that she had not sought for the Lord's confirmation of her husband's commitment and that she had entirely turned aside the message given her in the dream she had had at the Smith's home confirming the existence and the source of that sacred record.

But it is possible, however, to sympathize with Lucy. After participating in the hard work and the dangers of the settlement of Palmyra, she had reason to believe herself one of the most envied women of that area because of their present circumstances. "As might have been anticipated, Harris's wife became exceedingly annoyed and disgusted with what she called her husband's 'craziness.' She foresaw as she thought, that if he incurred the printing liability, as he had avowed to her his purpose of doing, the event would be the ruin of himself and family."[37] Furthermore, by this time Martin and Lucy were the parents of five children, and we may believe she thought she was defending their right to a more comfortable and secure existence than had been hers before this time. This alone could have led her to make an alliance with one, Flanders Dyke, whom she had before resisted as a future son-in-law. She now promised him her consent to marry her daughter Lucy if he helped her obtain the 116 pages of copied manuscript.

The several individuals who independently recounted the loss of the manuscript pages differ somewhat in details, but all agree that Martin's wife, Lucy, was the central figure in allowing the 116 pages to fall into the hands of "designing men."

His wife became more bitter and made it very uncomfortable for Martin. Finally, one day when a very dear friend dropped in to talk with him, he went to his room to get the manuscript to read it to his friend and unlocked the drawer where he had kept it. It was gone! Martin was now in a perplexing predicament. He searched every drawer, closet and nook and corner but without results. He worked himself into a frenzy, and when his wife returned home, she professed total ignorance as to their whereabouts. . . .

The manuscript mysteriously disappeared and was never found. There is a local story, or tradition, which runs as follows: When Joseph arrived from Harmony, Pa., he proceeded to the Harris farm on the following day, just as they were about to sit down for the noonday meal, and Joseph was asked to dine with them. During the course of the meal, the disappearance of the manuscript was brought up, and during the conversation something was said that piqued Mrs. Harris, who got up from the table quietly, went out the kitchen door and around to the front door, went upstairs into a bed-room where she had them hidden, put them in her apron, took them downstairs, walked into the north room and dumped them into the fireplace and burned them up.[38]

Thus exercised, she contrived in her husband's sleep to steal from him the particular source of her disturbance, and burned the manuscript to ashes. For years she kept this incendiarism a profound secret to herself even until after the book was published. Smith and Harris held her accountable for the theft, but supposed she had handed the manuscript to some "evil-designing persons" to be used somehow in injuring their cause. A feud was thus produced between husband and wife, which was never reconciled.[39]

Martin seems to have suffered temporally as well as spiritually for his transgression. The same day on which Martin reported to Joseph (then in Palmyra) the loss of the manuscript, "a dense fog spread itself over his fields, and blighted his wheat while in the blow, so that he lost about two-thirds of his crop, whilst those fields which lay only on the opposite side of the road, received no injury whatever."[40]

When Martin did not return soon to Harmony, Joseph, alarmed at his absence, followed him to Palmyra. Mother Smith invited Martin Harris to have breakfast with them. Her account is as follows:

At eight o'clock we set the victuals on the table, as we were expecting him every moment. We waited till nine, and he came not—till ten, and he was not there—till eleven, still he did not make his appearance. But at half past twelve we saw him walking with a slow and measured tread towards the house, his eyes fixed thoughtfully upon the ground. On coming to the gate, he stopped, instead of passing through, and got upon the fence, and sat there some time with his hat drawn over his eyes. At length he entered the house. Soon after which we sat down to the table, Mr. Harris with the rest. He took up his knife and fork as if he were going to use them, but immediately dropped them. Hyrum, observing this, said, "Martin, why do you not eat; are you sick?" Upon which Mr. Harris pressed his hands upon his temples, and cried out in a tone of deep anguish, "Oh, I have lost my soul! I have lost my soul!"

Joseph, who had not expressed his fears till now, sprang from the table, exclaiming, "Martin, have you lost the manuscript? Have you broken your oath, and brought down condemnation upon my head as well as your own?"

"Yes, it is gone," replied Martin, "and I know not where."

. . . . Said Joseph, clinching his hands. "All is lost! all is lost! What shall I do? I have sinned — it is I who tempted the wrath of God. I should have been satisfied with the first answer which I received from the Lord; for he told me that it was not safe to let the writing go out of my possession." He wept and groaned, and walked the floor continually.

At length he told Martin to go back and search again.

"No," said Martin, "it is all in vain; for I have ripped open beds and pillows; and I know it is not there."

"Then must I," said Joseph, "return with such a tale as this? I dare not do it. And how shall I appear before the Lord? Of what rebuke am I not worthy from the angel of the Most High?"[41]

The Lord's purposes will not be frustrated. He had provided for this circumstance in Book of Mormon days, when the great General Mormon instructed his son, Moroni, to finish the abridgement of the sacred records written by the prophets who had preceded them.. As it turned out, the record (1 Nephi through the Words of Mormon) was subsequently translated to replace the lost manuscript, thus giving more details than would have been printed otherwise, which is verified by the prophet's own statement: "To the reader . . . one hundred and sixteen pages the which I took from the Book of Lehi which was an account, abridged from the plates of Lehi by the hand of Mormon; which said account, some person or persons have stolen from me. . . . signed, Joseph Smith."[42]

The subsequent translation penned by Oliver Cowdery took seventy-five work days. He began writing for Joseph April 7 and completed the work at the end of June, 1829, at the Peter Whitmer farm in Fayette, New York. The Prophet had gone there in compliance with a revelation he had received, that wicked men were plotting to take his life. Joseph sent word of the completion of the translation to his parents in Palmyra. Joseph's mother wrote, "The same evening, we conveyed this intelligence to Martin Harris, for we loved the man, although his weakness had caused us much trouble."[43]

Although the Lord called Martin a "wicked man" for setting aside his pledge to show the manuscript to none other than those whom the Lord approved, it is evident that his repentance and remorse were sufficient to receive forgiveness and reinstatement into the Lord's grace. Martin Harris was favored in June, 1829, by being chosen as one of the Three Witnesses, along with Oliver Cowdery and David Whitmer, to the reality of the plates and the divinity of their message, as reported by Joseph. Martin Harris, Oliver Cowdery and David Whitmer had been most active in bringing forth the work, sacrificing both time and means. In a few days, according to the agreement, Martin arrived, bringing with him Joseph's father and mother. This was a very joyful occasion for each of them.

"On retiring to his room, Joseph humbly knelt in earnest supplication, asking the Lord to approve of his selection of these men who had contributed so much in bringing forth the work in which he was engaged. In answer to his prayers, the angel Moroni was sent to give instructions and arrange for the presentation of the plates before the three witnesses."[44]

At length the Prophet through the Urim and Thummim received from the Lord the following revelation directed to them:

> Behold, I say unto you, that you must rely upon my word, which if you do with full purpose of heart, you shall have a view of the plates, and also of the breastplate, the sword of Laban, the Urim and Thummim, which were given to the brother of Jared upon the mount, when he talked with the Lord face to face, and the miraculous directors which were given to Lehi while in the wilderness, on the borders of the Red Sea. And it is by your faih that you shall obtain a view of them, even by that faith which was had by the prophets of old. And after that you have obtained faith, and have seen them with your eyes, you shall testify of them, by the power of God; and this you shall do that my servant Joseph Smith, Jr., may not be destroyed, that I may bring about my righteous purpose unto the children of men in this work. And ye shall testify that you have seen them, even as my servant Joseph Smith, Jr., has seen them; for it is by my power that he has seen them, as it is because he had faith. And he has translated the book, even that part which I have commanded him,

and as your Lord and your God liveth it is true. Wherefore, you have received the same power, and the same faith, and the same gift like unto him; And if you do these last commandments of mine, which I have given you, the gates of hell shall not prevail against you; for my grace is sufficient for you; and you shall be lifted up at the last day. And I, Jesus Christ, your Lord and your God, have spoken it unto you, that I might bring about my righteous purposes unto the children of men. Amen. (D.&C. 5:11-13)

The day on which the Three Witnesses received their manifestation the usual morning family service was held at the Whitmer residence, namely, scripture-reading, singing, and prayer. Besides the Whitmer family, the Prophet and his wife and Oliver Cowdery, there were present the Prophet's father and mother and Martin Harris. As soon as Joseph rose from his knees, he approached Martin Harris and said, 'with a solemnity that thrills through my veins to this day,' says the Prophet's mother, who relates this circumstance: "Martin Harris, you have got to humble yourself before your God this day, that you may obtain a forgiveness of your sins. If you do, it is the will of God that you should look upon the plates in company with Oliver Cowdery and David Whitmer."

. . . Martin Harris, David Whitmer, Oliver Cowdery and myself, agreed to retire into the woods, and try to obtain, by fervent and humble prayer, the fulfillment of the promises given . . . that they should have a view of the plates. We accordingly made choice of a piece of woods convenient to Mr. Whitmer's house, to which we retired, and having knelt down, we began to pray in much faith to Almighty God to bestow upon us a realization of these promises.

According to previous arrangement, I commenced by vocal prayer to our Heavenly Father, and was followed by each of the others in succession. We did not at the first trial, however, obtain any answer or manifestation of divine favor in our behalf. We again observed the same order of prayer, each calling on and praying fervently to God in rotation, but with the same result as before.

Upon this, our second failure, Martin Harris proposed that he should withdraw himself from us, believing, as he expressed himself, that his presence was the cause of our not obtaining what we wished for. He accordingly withdrew from us, and we knelt down again, and had not been many minutes engaged in prayer, when presently we beheld a light above us in the air, of exceeding brightness; and behold, an angel stood before us. In his hands he held the plates which we had been praying for these to have a view of. He turned over the leaves one by one, so that we could see them, and discern the engravings thereon distinctly. He then addressed himself to David Whitmer, and said, "David, blessed is the Lord, and he that keeps His commandments;" when, immediately afterwards, we heard a voice from out of the bright light above us, saying, "These plates have been revealed by the power of God, and they have been translated by the power of God. The translation of them which you have seen is correct, and I command you to bear record of what you now see and hear."

I now left David and Oliver, and went in pursuit of Martin Harris, whom I found at a considerable distance, fervently engaged in prayer. He soon told me, however, that he had not yet prevailed with the Lord, and earnestly requested me to join him in prayer, that he also might realize the same blessings which we had just received. We accordingly joined in prayer, and ultimately obtained our desires, for before we had yet finished, the same vision was opened to our view, at least it was again opened to me, and I once more beheld and heard the same things: whilst at the same moment, Martin Harris cried out, apparently in an ecstasy of joy, "Tis enough; tis enough; mine eyes have beheld; mine eyes have beheld;" and jumping up, he shouted, "Hosanna," blessing God, and otherwise rejoiced exceedingly . . . [45]

It is well known that Martin's vision of the plates came to him near the Peter Whitmer farm in company with Joseph Smith, as Joseph withdrew from the other witnesses for prayer in Martin's behalf.

When Martin Harris came in, he seemed almost overcome with joy, and testified boldly to what he had both seen and heard. And so did David and Oliver, adding that no tongue could express the joy of their hearts and the greatness of the things which they had both seen and heard.

Having thus, through the mercy of God, obtained these glorious manifestations, it now remained for these three individuals to fulfill the commandment which they had received, viz., to bear record of these things; in order to accomplish which, they drew up and subscribed the following document:

THE TESTIMONY OF THREE WITNESSES

BE IT KNOWN unto all nations, kindreds, tongues, and people, unto whom this work shall come: That we, through the grace of God the Father, and our Lord Jesus Christ, have seen the plates which contain this record, which is a record of the people of Nephi, and also of the Lamanites, their brethren, and also of the people of Jared, who came from the tower of which hath been spoken. And we also know that they have been translated by the gift and power of God, for his voice hath declared it unto us; wherefore we know of a surety that the work is true. And we also testify that we have seen the engravings which are upon the plates; and they have been shown unto us by the power of God, and not of man. And we declare with words of soberness, that an angel of God came down from heaven, and he brought and laid before our eyes, that we beheld and saw the plates, and the engravings thereon; and we know that it is by the grace of God the Father, and our Lord Jesus

Christ, that we beheld and bear record that these things are true. And it is marvelous in our eyes. Nevertheless, the voice of the Lord commanded us that we should bear record of it; wherefore, to be obedient unto the commandments of God, we bear testimony of these things. And we know that if we are faithful in Christ, we shall rid our garments of the blood of all men, and be found spotless before the judgment seat of Christ, and shall dwell with him eternally in the heavens. And the honor be to the Father, and to the Son, and to the Holy Ghost, which is one God. Amen.[46]

Oliver Cowdery

David Whitmer

Martin Harris

"When the Angel [Moroni] made his departure, he took the plates with him and the Urim and Thummim."[47]

Soon after these things had transpired, a testimony was obtained from eight additional witnesses. According to Lucy Smith, these eight witnesses obtained a view of the plates near the Smith residence at Manchester.

Joseph Smith announced to his parents the relief he now felt at having witnesses to whom others could turn for verification of his claim.

To a gathering of friends during the later years of his life in Edward Stevenson's home, Martin Harris told what had occurred that day in Fayette, New York:

> . . . the angel stood on the opposite side of the table on which were the plates, the interpreters, etc.; and took the plates in his hand and turned them over. "To fully illustrate this to them, Brother Martin took up a book and turned the leaves over one by one." The angel declared that the Book of Mormon was correctly translated by the power of God . . . The witnesses were required to bear this testimony of these things and this open vision to all people . . . and before God, whom he expected to meet in the day of judgement, he lied not.[48]

The three witnesses wrote their testimony, which appears in each copy of the Book of Mormon, and offered their names to it at the Peter Whitmer farm in Fayette, New York.

Another positive evidence of Martin's being an eye witness is the account published in the *Deseret News' Church News*, October 9, 1982, p. 23, quoting a letter dictated by Martin Harris on January 13, 1873. This letter was located by Brent F. Ashworth, Provo, Utah. The text of the letter, with the original spelling, is as follows:

Smithfield
Cache Co. Utah
Jan 13th 1873

Brother Walter Conrad.

Dear Sir. — Your favor of the 7th inst. has been purused with much pleasure, and I am pleased to reply it is truly gratifying to hear of the continual increase of influence manifested by the Book of Mormon; and as you have entreated me to write my witness of said Book (and have graciously enclosed a stamp for the same) I now solemnly state that as I was praying unto the Lord that I might behold the ancient record, lo there appeared to view a holy Angel, and before him a table, and upon the table the holy spectacles or Urim and Thummim, and other ancient relics of the Nephites, and lo, the Angel did take up the plates, and turn them over so as we could plainly see th engravings thereon, and lo there came a voice from heaven saying "I am the Lord," and that the plates were translated by God and not by men, and also that we should bear record of it to all the world, and thus the vision was taken from us.

And now dear brother, I would that you might look upon my countenance and know that I lie not, neither was I deceived, but it pleases the Lord that I must be content to write these few lines.

Yours in the Gospel of Christ
Martin Harris

We are indebted to Martin Harris for the only detailed description of the gold plates. Martin told David B. Dille that on one occasion he had held the plates on his knee for an hour and a half while conversing with Joseph Smith. Martin also testified that every plate Joseph translated, he handled, plate after plate. "Describing their dimensions, he, Martin, pointed with his left hand to the back of his right hand and said, 'I should think they were so long, or about eight inches, and about so thick, or about four inches, and each of the plates was thinner than the thinnest tin.' "[49] According to Tiffany's monthly, published in 1859, Martin Harris gave the following description of the plates: "I hefted the plates many times and should think they weighed forty or fifty pounds." Martin also mentioned that the plates were kept in a cherry box made for that purpose.

Mother Smith told on page 104 of her book of the plans to have a chest made to secure the plates. She described the chest as being of red morocco, so perhaps the small trunk was of cherry wood covered with leather made from goatskin dyed with sumac, called Morocco.

It was now time for this sacred scripture to be given to the world. Joseph Smith first sought the services of Egbert B. Grandin, a young printer of Palmyra, in June 1829. Grandin, fearing he might become implicated with the unpopular group of people and their queer religious beliefs, refused to contract the job.

Joseph Smith then went to Rochester, New York, a distance of about thirty miles, and talked to Thurlow Weed, a shrewd politition and publisher of the *Rochester Telegraph*. But he also refused. The following day Joseph went again to Weed, accompanied by Martin Harris, who offered to be security for the expense of printing the unpopular book, but Weed declined a second time.

In the meantime, Grandin, according to tradition, consulted his family and friends and was convinced that printing a book was merely a business proposition and that he need not be connected with the religious beliefs of its author, so when Joseph and Martin again contacted Grandin, he consented to be the publisher. Martin mortgaged 240 acres of farm land to Grandin, in exhange for printing 5,000 copies.

This Indenture, Made the twenty fifth day of August in the year of our
Lord one thousand eight hundred and twenty nine between Martin Harris of the
town of Palmyra in the county of Wayne & State of New York, of the first part, and
Egbert B Grandin of the same place of the second part. Witnesseth, that the said
party of the first part for and in consideration of the Sum of three thousand dollars
to him in hand, paid by the said party of the second part, the receipt whereof is hereby
confessed and acknowledged, hath granted, bargained, sold, remised released,
enfeoffed and confirmed; and by these presents doth grant, bargain, sell, remise
release, enfeoff and confirm, unto the said party of the second part, and to his heirs and
assigns forever All that certain tract or parcel of Land situate in the said town
of Palmyra aforesaid bounded on the South by Lands belonging to Preserved Harris
on the east by Red Creek, on the north by Lands belonging to Emer Harris & the high-
way & on the west by the east line of the town of Macedon, being the same tract of
land or farm upon which the said Martin Harris now resides To have and to
hold the above bargained premises, to the said party of the second part, his heirs, and
assigns, to the sole and only proper use benefit and behoof of the said party of the second
part, his heirs and assigns forever Provided always, and these presents are upon this
express condition that if the said Martin Harris his heirs executors or administra-
trators shall pay or cause to be paid unto the said party of the second part his
heirs executors administrators or assigns the sum of three thousand dollars
at or before the expiration of eighteen months from the date hereof, then these
presents shall cease and be null and Void but in case of the nonpayment
of the said sum of Money, or any part thereof, at the times above limited
for the payment thereof, then and in such case it shall and may be lawful
for the said party of the second part, his heirs executors administrators or assigns
and the said party of the first part doth hereby empower and authorise the
said party of the second part his heirs executors, administrators or assigns
to grant, bargain sell, release and convey the said premises, or any part
or portion thereof with the appurtenances, at public auction or vendue
and on such sale to make and execute to the purchaser or purchasers
his or their heirs and assigns forever good ample or sufficient deed or
deeds of Conveyance in the law pursuant to the Statute in that case
made and provided — Rendering the Surplus Moneys (if any there should
be) to the said party of the first part his heirs, executors or administrators or assigns after deducting the costs and charges of such vendue and Sale
aforesaid. In witness whereof the party of the first part hath hereunto set
his hand and seal the day and year first above written. The nineteenth
and a part of the twentieth and twenty first lines obliterated before execution.

Signed Sealed and delivered in   Martin Harris. {seal}
the presence of   Fredk Smith

State of New York Wayne County ss. On the 26th day of August 1829 personally appeared before me Frederick Smith a Judge of Wayne County
the within grantor to me known to be the person described in, and
who executed the within deed & acknowledged that he executed the
same as his voluntary act and deed for the purposes therein contained
                                    Fredk Smith.

Part of the Mortgage Agreement between Martin Harris and Grandin.

In *The Prophet of Palmyra*, Gregg, a contemporary, relates:

> Upon my return to Palmyra and learning that Martin Harris was the only man of any account . . . , it was natural that I should seek an early interview with him. I found him at the printing office of the Wayne Sentinel in Palmyra, where the Book of Mormon was being printed.
>
> Here was a most remarkable quartette of persons. I soon learned that at least three of them were in daily attendance at the printing office, and that they came and went as regularly as the rising or setting of the sun.[50]
>
> The fact that such a man as Martin Harris should mortgage his farm for a large sum, to secure the publisher for printing the book, should abandon the cultivation of one of the best farms in the neighborhood and change all his habits of life . . . was truly phenomenal. He at the same time was the only man among all the primitive Mormons who was responsible in a pecuniary [monetary] sence for a single dollar. Nevertheless, he had become absolutely infatuated . . . If one passage more than another seemed to be in his mind it was this: "God has chosen the weak things of this world to confuse the wise."[51]

The mortgage was dated August 25, 1829.[52] The printing was begun that same month and was completed seven months later on March 26, 1830. Before printing began, Oliver Cowdery made a second copy of the valuable manuscript.

According to Willard Bean, who interviewed John H. Gilbert, the typesetter, a few pages of the copy were brought to the printing office daily by Hyrum Smith and Oliver Cowdery and taken home at night. It was written on foolscap paper in the good, clear handwriting of Cowdery. There was no punctuation in the entire manuscript. Therefore, it was not possible for the printers to set the type until these corrections were added. Names of persons and places

Grandin Building where first edition of the Book of Mormon was printed.

were capitalized, but the ampersand (&) was used throughout, and sentences had no end.

It is apparent that with Joseph's continuing dictation, Oliver had no time to determine the length of sentences or paragraphs, or needed punctuation, nor had Cowdery made any changes as he had recopied it.

Permission was granted Gilbert to take a few pages home each night for the purpose of adding correct punctuation. According to Joseph's mother, her son obtained a copyright from R.R. Lansing, clerk of the Northern District Court of New York on June 11, 1829.

The Book of Mormon was printed on a new Smith Press acquired by the publisher for this large order, which exceeded by 3,000 copies the amount usually contracted.

The press was on the third floor of the Grandin Building located at 219 Main Street in Palmyra. Binding was done on the second floor.

Typesetters are said to have worked eleven hours a day, six days a week for seven months until the book was finally completed on March 26, 1830.

As Grandin began the printing he advertised for sheepskins sufficient in number to make 5,000 leather bound covers for this new book of scripture.

On March 26, 1830, Grandin's newspaper, *The Wayne Sentinal*, contained an advertisement for the Book of Mormon, mentioning the fact that the book contained 600 pages, large duodecimo, and was now for sale, wholesale and retail, at the Palmyra Bookstore, by E.B. Grandin, "on the ground floor of said building."

Some may wish to know why Joseph Smith, Jr., was called "author and proprietor" in the 1830 edition.

In those days the copyright laws would not permit printing of any translated material, so an author had to be named. This is explained in *History of the Church*, Vol. I, p. 58.

The *Palmyra Courier* reported: "Shortly after the completion of the printing of the Book of Mormon, Martin Harris began (his effort) to sell the work, and was daily seen on the street, inviting his friends and neighbors to buy. His

Martin given permission by Joseph Smith to sell the Book of Mormon.

form was conspicuous, with a grey suit of homespun, his head surmounted by a large stiff hat, while under his arm he carried several copies of the book."[53]

It is common knowledge that the Book of Mormon was not accepted in the Palmyra area, even though sincere effort was made to sell it. It was to be sold for not less than 10 shillings ($1.25 in 1830). Martin didn't sell a single copy.

> Harris was proverbially a peaceful as well as an honest man. He was slow to retaliate an offense. Urging the sale of the book . . . he fell into debate about its character with a neighbor . . . His opponent became angry and struck him a severe blow upon the right side of his face.

> Instantly turning toward the assailant the other cheek, he [Harris] quoted the Christian maxim, reading it from the book in his hand [Book of Mormon] page 481 [as it also appears in Matthew 5:39], "Whosoever shall smite thee on the right cheek, turn to him the other."[55]

With the completion of the printing project, friends and relatives began requesting baptism. In conformity with previous arrangements, Joseph Smith called a meeting to organize the Church, which would be called "The Church of Jesus Christ."

This important event took place at the home of Peter Whitmer in Fayette, Seneca County, New York, on April 6, 1830. The law required that there must be at least six members who held beliefs in common. On that same day several more believers requested baptism, which was by immersion. "Old Mr. Smith and Martin Harris came forrod [forward] to be Babtise[d] for the first. They found a place in a . . . small Stream ran thro and they ware Babtized in the Evening Bcause of persecution. They went forward and was Babtized. Being the first I saw Babtised in the new and everlasting Covenant."[56]

When Martin Harris dictated some of the events of his life to Edward Stevenson, he stated, "Then I was baptized . . . being the first after Joseph & Oliver."[57]

Christina Graves Granger, with the famous money belt draped around her neck.

"Joseph was fild with the Spirrit to a grate Degree to see his father and Mr. Harris that he had bin with so much he Bast [burst] out with greaf and joy and seamed as tho the world could not hold him . . . He . . . appeared to want to git out of site of every Body and would sob and Crie and seamed to be so full . . . "[58]

When the mortgage on Martin's farm fell due in eighteen months, there was no money to pay it. Meanwhile, a Thomas Lakey had purchased the note from E.B. Grandin. In 1831, Mrs. Christina Graves Grainger, a widow, found her way to Palmyra from England, accompanied by her father and four children. Mrs. Grainger brought with her $3,000.00 in gold coins secured in a money belt fastened around her waist, and with that money paid Mr. Lakey and took possession of the farm.

> The said Martin Harris, for the consideration hereinafter mentioned, agrees to sell to the said Thomas Lakey the farm on which he now resides, containing by estimation, one hundred and fifty acres, for the sum of twenty dollars for each acre, and, forthwith to obtain a correct survey of said premises, and give a good warranty deed of same, and give immediate possession of everything. Always excepting and reserving the privilege of living in the house till the first of May next. The said Thomas Lakey is to have all the wheat on the ground except ten acres sown by Mr. Dyke, and the one-half of the said ten acres shall belong to the said Thomas Lakey after the said Dyke shall harvest the same and shock it up in the field.

> In consideration whereof, the said Thomas Lakey agrees to pay to the said Martin Harris, one third of the purchase money on the first day of next May, and one third in the month of October next, and the remaining one third in the month of October in the year eighteen hundred and thirty-two. In consideration whereof the parties bind themselves in the penal sum of five hundred dollars, begin damages assessed and agreed upon by the

parties. In witness wereof, the parties have hereunto interchangeably set their hands and seals, the day and year first above writen.

(signed)
MARTIN HARRIS, L.S.
THOMAS LAKEY, L.S.

. . . the same tract of land or farm upon which the said Martin Harris now resides. To have and to hold the above bargained premises.[59]

The frame home which Martin had built early in his married life was now lost because of the mortgage default. As originally built, it had one and one-half stories and probably as many as nine rooms. It was of frame construction and painted white, which was unusual in that area. In 1849, it burned to the ground. The new owner, William Chapman, who was now the second husband of Christiana Graves Grainer, immediately made plans for a new one.

It was built upon the same foundation and consequently included the walled-up rock basement of the original building, the walls being those constructed by Joseph Smith, Sr., and his son Hyrum.

This farm home has outer walls composed of washed lake stones obtained from the shores of Lake Ontario, which is twenty miles distance from Palmyra. It was necessary for those to be brought by ox-team. The trip required three days; one to reach the lake, one to obtain the rock, and one to make the return trip. The veneer is made of carefully sized stones, made so by thrusting them through a wire ring of a given size, or a hole in a board. The outside walls are twenty-six inches thick.

This unique cobblestone art died with its builders, as they would not permit any onlookers when working and refused to pass on any of their trade secrets. This prestige-ous home is known as a typical but rare cobblestone house, being one of over seven hundred in or near this region. The builders came originally from England. The homes are reminiscent of the Roman Empire and medieval France.[60]

The home and eighty-eight acres of the original farm were purchased by the LDS Church in 1937 as a visitor's center in recognition of the sacrifice Martin Harris had made.

There is no authoritative source to indicate that Martin Harris was ever reimbursed completely for the sale of his property, but over twenty years later Mr. Dille recorded: "I then asked Mr. Harris if he ever lost three thousand dollars by the publishing of the Book of Mormon. Mr. Harris said, 'I never lost one cent. Mr. Smith paid me all that I advanced and more too.' " The Prophet was in such financial straits from the beginning of his life to his martyrdom that these payments must have been mainly figurative. Martin Harris was never known to express regret at his sacrifice for the printing of the books.

When Martin's property was about to be sold, his wife, Lucy, left him, taking their children, and never again returned to live with Martin Harris. She occupied the property he had previously deeded her.

Chapter III

Recompensed and Rejected

Almost immediately after the organization of the Church, persecutions broke out anew. Before many months the Prophet took his family and moved to Kirtland, Ohio. From the writings of Joseph Smith we learn that they left Fayette, New York, in the latter part of January, 1831, and arrived at the home of Newel K. Whitney, a baptized member, the first part of February, 1831.

While Martin was still in Palmyra, New York, Joseph Smith sent him a letter dated February 22, 1831, from Kirtland, Ohio, stating in part as follows: "I send you this to inform you that it is necessary for you to come here as soon as you can in order to choose a place to settle on which may be best adapted to the circumstances of your life . . . you may choose any place that may best suit yourselves anywhere in this part of the country . . . you will also bring or cause to be brought all the books [meaning undoubtedly copies of the Book of Mormon] . . . you will not sell the books for less than 10 shillings."[62]

The *Wayne Sentinel* reported the following:

> Several families, numbering about fifty souls, took up their line of march from this town last week for the promised land, among whom was Martin Harris, one of the original believers in the "Book of Mormon." Mr. Harris was among the early settlers of this town, and has ever borne the character of an honorable and upright man, and an obliging and benevolent neighbor. He had secured to himself by honest industry a respectable fortune, and he has left a large circle of acquaintances and friends to pity his delusions.[63]

Two groups of Latter-day Saints had gone on to the Ohio by this time. "A third group, about fifty members from Palmyra, New York, left May 27, 1831, for Buffalo on the Erie Canal which ran through their village. Led by Martin Harris, they arrived in Kirtland in June."[64]

Martin Harris no doubt had made his choice of property as requested by the Prophet, but his stay in Kirtland was extremely short, since at a conference held at Kirtland June 7, 1831, Missouri was designated as the place for the next conference, and many of the stalwarts of the Church were called to gather: "Let my servant Joseph Smith, Jr. and Sidney Rigdon take their journey as soon as possible to the land of Missouri. And inasmuch as they are faithful unto me it shall be made known unto them what they shall do; and again let my servant Edward Partridge and Martin Harris take their journey with my servants Sidney Rigdon and Joseph Smith, Jr" (D&C 52:24).

Joseph Smith recorded:

> On the 19th June in company with Sidney Rigdon, Martin Harris . . . I started from Kirtland, Ohio for the land of Missouri agreeable to the commandments before received wherein it was promised that if we were faithful, the land of our inheritance, even the place for the city of the New Jerusalem, should be revealed. We went by wagon, canal boats, and stages to Cincinnati. We left Cincinnati in a steamer and landed at Louisville, Kentucky, where we were detained three days in waiting for a steamer to convey us to St. Louis. At St. Louis myself, brother Harris, Phelps, Partridge and Coe went by land on foot to Independence, Jackson County, Missouri where we arrived about the middle of July, and the rest of the company came by water a few days later.[65]

On August 1, 1831, the first Sabbath after this group arrived in Jackson County, Missouri, they desired to know the will of the Lord through the Prophet. The Lord gave the following:

> Behold, verily I say unto you, for this cause I have sent you that you might be obedient, and that your hearts might be prepared to bear the testimony of the things which are to come; And also that you might be honored in laying the foundation and in bearing record of the land upon which the Zion of God shall stand. . . .

It is wisdom in me that my servant Martin Harris should be an example unto the Church, in laying his moneys before the bishop of the church. . . .

And let him repent of his sins, for he seeketh the praise of the world. (D&C 58:6-7, 35, 39)

This was the third such call to this man for his means. Section 19 of the Doctrine and Covenants, dated March, 1830, is devoted entirely to instructions given to Martin Harris the previous year. He was instructed again to impart his property freely as he had done for the publication of the Book of Mormon: "Impart a portion of thy property, yea, even part of thy lands, and all save the support of thy family. . . . Leave thy house and home, except when thou shalt desire to see thy family" (D&C 19:34, 36).

Independence, Missouri, was to be the center place of Zion, to which the Saints should gather. Martin Harris was present when the temple lot was dedicated there on August 3, 1831, and no doubt was one of the main contributors to the subsequent purchase.

The group returned August 27, 1831, to Kirtland, Ohio. After several meetings, it was concluded that the revelations should be printed in book form, and Martin Harris was selected with four others to manage the business of getting this accomplished. These men were warned that an account of this stewardship would be required on the Day of Judgment (See D&C 70:1, 3–4): "(Special conference, Hiram, Portage, Ohio November 12, 1831) Brother Martin has labored with me from the beginning . . . for a considerable time and as these sacred writings are now going to the Church for its benefit . . . [The conference voted] that Brother Joseph Smith Junior be appointed to dedicate and consecrate these brethren and the sacred writings and all they have entrusted to their care, to the Lord."[66]

Martin's whereabouts for the next two years is uncertain, but on January 25, 1832, his brother, Emer, and Simeon Carter were called to "be united in the ministry" (D&C 75:30). At some point the Harris brothers began laboring together. The result of their missionary effort reads: "Dec. 21, 1832 . . . brothers Martin and Emer Harris have baptized 100 persons at Chenango point, (South of Oneida Lake) New York, within a few weeks past. Newel [Knight]."[67]

A letter from Emer Harris dated May 7, 1833, from Springville, Pennsylvania, addressed to The Brethren in Brownhelm, Lorain County, Ohio, states:

> Brother Martin is with me & has been the grater part of the time since we left Kirtland. We have traveled mutch & Preached mutch. Eighty-two have been baptized and many more have believed. We find no end to the call for our labours. And many miracles have been done in the Name of Jesus Christ & signs follow them at believe. . . .
>
> The 24th of Last January Bro Martin was taken a prisoner on a fals charge . . . & went to prison a few days until we got Bail to answer to Cort . . . but it is now put over until the next September tirm . . . thither we cannot tell when we will be expected in the Ohio.[68]

Included with the foregoing letter was this poem:

(To Brother Martin Harris)

1. Dear Brother though you are bound in jail
   Yet never fear the powers of hell
   Your God he will deliver you
   Therefore fear not what men can do.

2. He can deliver you as Paul
   If its to brake the prison wall
   And let the jaylor see
   He is a God of majisty

3. And those that have by wicked hands
   Have disobeyed the Lords commands
   They must repent or they will go
   To extreme misery and wo.

4. They've took a servant of the Lord
   And disobeyed the word of God
   And put him in the silent jail
   But he will pray in spite of hell

5. Dear souls repent and turn to God
   Or you shall feel his angry nod
   And he will shut the mercy dore
   And you be lost for ever more.

6. Behold you're trampling on his word
   When you so slight this work of God
   Therefore repent and do not say
   That revelations are done away.

7. But for revenge we will not seek
   Hear what the word of God doth speak
   Vengence is mine I will repay
   Therefore repent without delay.

8. Repent I say repent and hear
   Behold I warn you in God's fear
   Or you at the great rising day
   Shall hear the word depart away.

9. Let all the hosts of hell engauge
   With all their mallice spite and rage
   The Mormonites God will defend
   Who are so called by wicked men.[68]

On February 17, 1834, Martin Harris, having now returned, was chosen a member of the first high council of the Church in Kirtland, Ohio. Later in that same year he became a member of Zion's Camp, composed of 150 men who were to go to Jackson County, Missouri, in behalf of the Church members there who were being "afflicted, and persecuted" because of their "contentions, and envyings . . . and covetous desires" (D&C 101:1, 6):

> Individuals who experienced this march recorded this incident:
>
> Martin Harris having boasted to the brethren that he could handle snakes with perfect safety, while fooling with a black snake with his bare feet, he received a bite on his left foot. . . .
>
> Joseph Smith reproved him for trifling with the promises of God "when the circumstance is unnecessary."[69]

When Zion's Camp arrived, they were unable to fulfill their purpose. Governor Dunklin was unwilling to reinstate the people in their lands. The camp was disbanded June 24, 1834, as their presence had inflamed the minds of the Missourians and a civil war could have resulted. The Church members there had lost much in property, but the experiences proved a test of faith for all involved as well as preparatory training for their great exodus to the West.

On February 14, 1835, Joseph Smith called a special meeting of those who had served in Zion's Camp and invited other Saints who wished to attend. President Smith said that the first business of the meeting was for the Three Witnesses of the Book of Mormon — Oliver Cowdery, David Whitmer and Martin Harris—to pray, each one, and then proceed to choose twelve men from the Church As apostles, to go to all nations, kindreds, tongues, and people.

The Three Witnesses united in prayer. They were then blessed by the laying on of hands by the Presidency. The Witnesses then, according to the former commandment, proceeded to make choice of the Twelve.[70]

Nine of the Twelve then chosen had been members of Zion's Camp. On one occasion Martin's enthusiasm for the establishment of the Restored Church was manifest in a rash statement that prompted Joseph Smith to reprimand Martin and also to utter an interesting prophecy. Isaac Decker related the incident as follows:

> In 1836, soon after the dedication of the Kirtland Temple, and while the brethren were holding meetings from house to house, breaking bread, concecrating and drinking wine and prophesying, I attended one of the meetings where Joseph Smith, Martin Harris and John Smith were present. Martin said there would not be a living Gentile on the earth in four years. Joseph reproved him and said, "Brother Martin, you are too fast. After messages are sent with lightning speed from the east to the west sea and an Iron track from one side of the

world to the other, with iron carriages drawn by iron horses snorting fire and smoke, with less speed than the messages are carried, then it may do to talk about the time for the destruction of the Gentiles. But before that takes place they will make wonderful improvements in machinery of every kind, especially implements of husbandry for the working of the land and raising grain, saving a great deal of labor to the Saints in building up the kingdom. The Lord will inspire the Gentiles to do this, but they will not acknowledge his hand in it, nor give him the glory, but will take the glory to themselves, and when the destruction comes the wicked will slay the wicked; the Saints will not destroy the Gentiles, they will be divided among themselves and destroy one another. But the time is with the Lord. The benefits of all the ingenuity and inventions will be the means of advancing the building up of Zion with greater speed. The Lord will have the glory."[71]

Mary Elizabeth Rollins Lightner related the following experience, which occurred during the Kirtland, Ohio, period:

[One night] Mother and I went to the Smith house. There were other visitors. As we stood talking to them, Brother Joseph and Martin Harris came in. It was the first time some of them had ever seen the Prophet. He then said. "There are enough here to hold a little meeting."

A board was put across two chairs to make seats. Martin Harris sat on a box at Joseph's feet. They sang and prayed; then Joseph got up to speak. He began very solemnly and very earnestly. All at once his countenance changed and he stood mute. He turned so white he seemed perfectly transparent. Those who looked at him that night said he looked like he had a searchlight within him, in every part of his body. I remember I thought we could almost see the bones through the flesh on his face. . . .

He stood some moments looking over the congregation, as if to pierce each heart, then said, "Do you know who has been in your midst this night?"

One of the Smiths said, "An angel of the Lord?"

Joseph did not answer. Martin Harris was sitting at the Prophet's feet on a box. He slid to his knees, clasped his arms around the Prophet's knees and said, "I know, it is our Lord and Savior, Jesus Christ!"

Joseph put his hand on Martin's head and answered, "Martin, God revealed that to you. Brothers and Sisters the Savior has been in your midst this night. . . . He has given you all to me, and commanded me to seal you up to everlasting life, that where He is there you may be also."

Then he knelt and prayed and such a prayer I never heard, before or since. I felt he was talking to the Lord, and the power rested upon us all.[72]

A patriarchal blessing was given to Martin by his close friend of years past, Joseph Smith, Sr., on August 27, 1835. The blessing is quoted here in part:

Thou art a son of Zion and hast consecrated thy all for the good of her, yea thou hast greatly desired her deliverence and her welfare. Thou must be humble and meek in heart or Satan will seek to raise thee up to pride and boasting . . . Thou hast left thy family and house for the Gospels sake and given all for the purpose of spreading the word of thy God . . . yea thou hast left thy family and consecrated them unto the Lord and if thou desirest it with all thy heart and art faithful, thou yet shall teach them even thy wife that she may be saved in the day of eternity, but if not they shall be removed from the earth, and their place shall be supplied with another and thy heart shall be satisfied, for thou shalt raise up seed unto the Lord to praise him in his Kingdom.[73]

Work on the Kirtland Temple had commenced in June 1833, while Martin was waiting to be released from the charges made against him in Pennsylvania. At that time, according to Heber C. Kimball, "The church was in a state of poverty and distress, in consequence of which it appeared almost impossible that the commandment (to build the temple) could be fulfilled. . . ."[74]

Modern visitors to the Kirtland Temple are told by the guides there that the Saints were given the rubble from a nearby stone quarry at a very reduced price for taking it away. It was necessary then to finish the outside walls of the temple with a plaster coat to cover the irregular stone from which it was constructed. The temple was completed and dedicated March 27, 1836.

Shortly after the completion of the temple, Joseph Smith and Martin Harris took a short tour through the eastern country, arriving at Palmyra in 1836.[75] No doubt Martin made a last attempt to reconcile with Lucy and the children. During the summer of that same year, Martin's wife, Lucy, from whom he had been separated for five years (there is no record of a divorce), died in Palmyra. She lies buried in The Gideon Durphey Cemetery, Palmyra, New York.

It must have been about this time that Martin Harris built his commodious and lovely home in Kirtland, Ohio, which at the time of this writing stands as a reminder of the Lord's blessings upon him. This house is located in a beautiful wooded area about one and one-half miles east from the city. It is constructed of evenly cut, slate-colored stone, sturdy and somber.

Other homes of this era were less substantial. The growth of the Church had been rapid. The numbers living in that vicinity soon exceeded by several times the numbers residing in the New York and Pennsylvania branches. This land, of course, was thought to be their "Zion," but nevertheless, the newly converted who arrived almost daily were for the greater part financially unable to erect desirable permanent dwellings. One case, not necessarily an isolated one, is that of Amasa M. Lyman, who, after his

Martin Harris Home in Kirtland, Ohio as seen in March 1978.

conversion, walked a distance of nearly seven hundred miles and arrived almost penniless. The members as a whole were poor, having sold, upon short notice and sometimes with promised future payments, the greater part of their accumulated properties. Others who were more fortunate were inclined to use their surplus on land speculation. Newel K. Whitney early operated a store in Kirtland, Ohio known as the Gilbert and Whitney Mercantile. He was considered a successful young man, but it was necessary for him to use a portion of this small two-story, wooden building as his home. Even though one sees today a prestigious white frame building designated as the Sidney Rigdon home directly across the street from the Kirtland Temple, this originally consisted of three rooms of roughly hewn logs.

Martin married Caroline Young, daughter of John Young (Brigham Young's brother) on November 1, 1836, at Kirtland, Geauga, Ohio, Heber C. Kimball officiated. (In her old age Caroline gave the date as 1837, but this would be incorrect, as Heber C. Kimball was in England on a mission in 1837.)

In 1837 there began the chain of events that led to Martin's long separation from the Church. A massive apostasy from the Church took place in 1837-38. Some left the Church and others were excommunicated. The failure of the Kirtland Safety Society was a main contributing factor. Some Church members had assumed that because Joseph Smith was treasurer and Sidney Rigdon secretary, the society could not fail.

At the failure of The Kirtland Safety Society, the Prophet especially was censored. It was reported that the 'bank' had been 'instituted by the will of God,' i.e., by revelation, 'and would never fail, let man do what they would.' This the Prophet denied in open conference, saying that'if this had been declared no one had authority from him for doing so;' and added that he 'had always said that unless the institution was conducted on righteous principles it would not stand.' Many, however, became disaffected toward the Prophet, 'as though I were the sole cause,' . . . he writes, 'of those very evils I was most strenuously striving against and which were actually brought upon us by the brethren not giving heed to my council.'[76]

A conference was held September 3, 1837, in the Kirtland Temple for the purpose of sustaining Church Officers. Brigham Young asked the faithful Saints to attend so that the officers in good standing might be sustained by the vote of the people.[77] The Saints rejected four members of the stake high council, including Martin Harris.

According to one account, Martin was disfellowshipped "for speaking against the Prophet."[78] However, it is not clear just what other action, if any, was taken regarding Martin's standing.

John Smith, who at the time was a sustained assistant to Joseph Smith, stated in a letter from Kirtland, dated January 1, 1838, that between forty and fifty people, including Martin, were cut off from the Church.[79] However, Brigham Young stated at a later date: "Martin Harris felt greatly disappointed, that he was not called to leadership, but Martin Harris never denied the faith, never affiliated with any other sect or denomination, . . . It is true that Martin Harris did not apostatize; he was never tried for his fellowship; he was never excommunicated."[80]

In the early days of the Church (only seven or eight years old then) the policies and procedures for excommunication or disfellowship were vague and vacillating. Some members were cut off from the Church for swearing or whipping their horses, some for speaking ill of Church leaders.

In addition to Martin's censure at the conference in Kirtland, on September 1837, "the following may have shattered his weakened alliance to the struggling Church structure. On May 23, 1841, at the conference held at Kirtland, Ohio, the acceptance by the members of the High Priests Quorum were voted upon. All six men were accepted unanimously but our brother, Martin Harris, who was rejected because there was one vote against him."[81]

In an account by Justin Brooks we find: "Nov. 7, 1842 Kirtland, Ohio. Twelve persons were baptized yesterday and information has just reached me that Brother Martin Harris has been baptized and is now on his way home from the water."[82] However, it is well known that hundreds of early Church members were baptized more than once when they or their leaders thought it necessary. This rebaptism illustrates a belief that baptism is a cleansing process. Rebaptism was also used as proof of committment to a specific principle, such as the United Order.

Martin appears to have been affiliated with several dissenting sects after the deaths of Joseph and Hyrum Smith, but when questioned about his intentions in England as an associate of James J. Strang, Martin stated, "No man heard me in any way deny the truth of the Book of Mormon; the administration of the angel that showed me the plates; nor the organization of the Church of Jesus Christ of Latter-day Saints under the administration of Joseph Smith."[83] When several men called the Book of Mormon nonsense, Martin bore testimony of its truthfulness and said "all would be damned if they rejected it."[84]

It is known that Martin Harris went on a mission to Great Britain as an associate of James J. Strang, apostate who claimed to be Joseph Smith's rightful successor. On arrival of a group of Strang's followers, the *Millennial Star*, as was its right, published several articles warning the people against them. In Birmingham, England, before a group of Latter-day Saints, Martin introduced himself and wished to speak, but his offer was rejected. When we came out of the meeting, Martin Harris was beset with a crowd in the street, expecting that he would furnish them with material to war against Mormonism, but when he was asked if Joseph Smith was a true Prophet of God, he answered "yes"; and when asked if the Book of Mormon was true, this was his answer: "Do you know that [it] is the sun shining on us? Because as sure as you know that, I know that Joseph Smith was a true prophet of God, and that he translated that book by the power of God."[85]

It appears that he may have become ashamed of his Strang affiliations so he stated that he was of the same faith as they, and at every opportunity while in Great Britain, he confined his remarks to the coming forth of the Book of Mormon and his witness of its truth.

At one time Martin was questioned about his "Strangite" mission to England which he answered in the following manner: "Question 1. Did you go to England to lecture against 'Mormonism'? I answer emphatically no, I did not. No man heard me in any way deny the truth of the Book of Mormon, the administration of the angel that showed me the plates; nor the organization of the Church of Jesus Christ of Latter-day Saints under the administration of Joseph Smith, Jr."[86]

To some it was known that before 1855, Martin's short interest in Shakerism came to an end. It has been said that he was briefly attracted to the belief held in common of revelations, and visitation of angels.

The movement of William E. M'Lellin and the Whitmerites claimed Martin Harris' attention during the next ten years. By 1858 he had had his fill and was inclined to follow William Smith and the Church of Christ. It is easy to understand why, after the death of the Prophet and Hyum Smith, Martin was inclined to accept this man as the rightful leader of the Church, as his love and association with the Smith family was of long-standing. He had preserved his association with them. The following is indicative of the regard in which they held Martin during the Kirtland period.

Joseph and his brother, William had quarreled, and a spirit of disunity existed in the family. On New Year's Day, 1836, William, Hyrum, and Joseph Smith, Sr., in company with John Smith, an uncle of the Prophet, and Martin Harris, went to the Joseph Smith home. Under the tender guidance of these men, William and Joseph discussed their differences and asked each other's forgiveness. It was a spiritual and solemn occasion, recorded in detail in the *History of the Church* by Joseph Smith, Jr., under the date of January 1, 1836.

"Martin had in his possession the keys to the Kirtland Temple and was its self appointed caretaker. With reverence, he conducted visitors through that holy edifice."

Chapter IV

Disdained and Dishonored

Little would be known of Martin Harris during the time he separated himself from the Church if it weren't for the reports of missionaries from the West who visited with him in Kirtland, Ohio. All seem to have seen in him bitterness and discord with the Church, but when the Book of Mormon was mentioned or questions were asked about its authenticity, he immediatly came to its defense and bore testimony of its truth and related those experiences in which he had played a part. During this time Martin had in his possession the keys to the Kirtland Temple and was its self-appointed caretaker. With reverence, he conducted visitors through that holy edifice.

The storm of apostasy which had ravaged the Church had certainly swept Martin Harris in its grasp, but his name has never been found on the rolls of any of the aforementioned groups as an actual member. The vacillation that beset him for the next thirty-two years must have been almost beyond human endurance, and it seems he had been warned of such distress, as recorded in Doctrine and Covenants 19:33: "And misery thou shalt receive if thou wilt slight these counsels, yes, even the destruction of thyself and property."

It seems that some of his problems might not have existed if he had been in full accord at the time when the more valiant Church members moved on to Missouri, and had accompanied them to Nauvoo, as it was there that many revelations and much counsel were expounded by Joseph Smith, especially as pertained to Church organization and doctrine.

David B. Dille recorded in his diary in the spring of 1853 that a visit with Martin found him bitter against the Church and against polygamy in particular; but when it was explained to him, he indicated understandig: "It is so, but I never thought of it in that light before. You have brought the old spirit of Mormonism here. He said to me 'Do I not know the Book of Mormon is true? Did I not hear the voice of God out of Heaven declaring that it was truth and correctly translated? Yes, I did.' "[87]

Lorenzo Snow reported somewhat the same experience with Martin Harris in 1855. Martin spoke of his uncertainties, finding no satisfaction with other groups: "[He] concluded he would wait until the Saints returned to Jackson County and then he would repair there."[88] The interview was concluded by Martin's testimony of the coming forth of the Book of Mormon.

In the 1860 census of Kirtland, Ohio, Martin was listed in the household of his son George. Here Martin gave his occupation as "Mormon Preacher."

These must have been heartbreaking years for Martin's wife, Caroline, who had married him when he was in full fellowship in the Church. By the time their first child was born, he had begun to be numbered with the "rappers," and nineteen years of uncertainty followed.

Caroline, a faithful member of the Church, urged her husband for years to join the migration to the Rocky Mountains, where most of the Saints had preceded them. There her heart strings pulled her, where her family, with Uncle Brigham and most of her friends, now had their homes. But Martin stubbornly refused to listen to her entreaties. In final desperation she resolutely took matters into her own hands and left her well-to-do husband, as Martin Harris was considered at that time. Caroline decided in favor of poverty and hardships, as contrasted with her former comfort and security.

With indomitable courage, she forsook the sanctuary of her Kirtland home and with her four children started the trek westward. Heavy in pregnancy, she was forced to stop at Pottawattamie County, Iowa, where Ida May, the youngest daughter, was born May 27, 1856. Making her weary way westward, as circumstances permitted, she finally reached the Missouri River and joined the ox-team caravan of Captain H.D. Haight, which arrived in Salt Lake City, Utah, on September 1, 1859, more than three years after Caroline had left Kirtland. She and her children were warmly welcomed into her father's home in Salt Lake City.[89]

A few months after Caroline and her children arrived, she married a widower, John Catley Davis, January 16, 1860. He was said to be "an associate of the Prophet," a skilled locksmith and gunsmith, a man of good repute who had joined the Church in Birmingham, England. His wife, Phebe Oxenbold, had died crossing the plains and left seven children. We find no record of a divorce of Caroline from Martin Harris. However, one could correctly assume that the laws of the frontier at this time gave Caroline proper license for her remarriage. According to recorded statements, when a three year period of time had elapsed during which a woman had received no support from her husband, she was legally free to contract another marriage.[90]

Three months later, Caroline's eldest daughter, Julia Lacothia, planned to marry one of Mr. Davis' sons, Elijah W. Davis. Subsequently, they were accompanied to the Endowment House by their parents, Caroline and John, and the latter, as well as the young couple, were sealed on March 1, 1860.[91]

We know very little of Caroline and John's life together except that a child was born to Caroline on November 19, 1860, in Payson, Utah. The child was named Joseph Harris Davis, but he lived only two days. When they returned to Salt Lake, they resided in the 17th Ward.[92]

The marriage finally ended unhappily: "Tradition has it that a dispute over land ownership arose between John Catley Davis and Brigham Young, and Caroline sided with her Uncle Brigham, rather than with her husband. . . . The altercation led to the separation of Caroline and Davis.[93] Caroline resumed the name of Harris."[94]

After the separation, Mr. Davis went to Pleasant Grove, where he made his home with his daughter Elizabeth Davis Stewart.

From a granddaughter, Mrs. Atwood, we learn that Mr. Davis started from Pleasant Grove to go to Idaho to visit his other children. When he arrived in Brigham City he became ill. He died February 16, 1878 at Brigham City, Utah.

CLAIM OF WIDOW FOR BOUNTY LAND.

N. B.—All the blank spaces in this form must be carefully filled up in accordance with the instructions on the back hereof; and from the best information possessed, or obtainable, by the applicant.

18 Aug 1879

State of *Utah*   County of *Cache* , SS.

On this *eighteenth* day of *August*, A. D. one thousand eight hundred and *seventy nine*, personally appeared before me, *Clerk of the County Court for Cache* the same being a **court of record** within and for the county and State aforesaid (1) *Caroline Harris*, aged *63* years, a resident of *Smithfield*, in the State of *Utah*, who, being duly sworn according to law, declares that she is the widow of (2) *Martin Harris* deceased, who was the identical (3) *Harris* , who served under the name of (4) *Martin Harris* as a (5) *Private* in the company commanded by Captain *Durfee* in the *N. York* regiment of *Militia*, commanded by *Ziri Leib*, in the war of (6) *1812* ; that her said husband was drafted at *Palmyra, N.Y.* on or about the _____ day of _____ , A. D. *1813*, for the term of _____, and continued in actual service in said war for the term of (8) *William Says*, and whose services terminated, by reason of (9) *the close of the War*, at _____, on the _____ day of _____, A. D. *1813*. She further states that the following is a full description of her said husband at the time of his enlistment, viz: (10) *he was about five feet eight inches high, light complectioned, blue eyes*. She further states that she was married to the said *Martin Harris*, at the city (or town) of *Kirtland*, in the county of *Lake*, and in the State of *Ohio*, on the *First* day of *November* A. D. *1857* by one (11) *Heber C. Kimball* who was a (12) *Minister*; and that her name before her said marriage was *Caroline Young*; and she further states that (13) *said Martin Harris had previously been married to Lucy Harris who died at Palmyra N.Y. in 1837*. and that her said husband (14) *Martin Harris*, died at *Clarkston* in the State of *Utah*, on the *tenth* day of *July* A. D. *1875*; and she further declares that the following have been the places of residence of herself and her said husband since the date of his discharge from the Army, viz: (15) *Palmyra N.Y. Kirtland Ohio, Smithfield & Clarkston, Utah* She makes this declaration for the purpose of obtaining the bounty land (or the additional bounty land) to which she may be entitled under the act approved March 3, 1855, and hereby appoints *William Bell, Washington* of _____, her true and lawful Attorney, to prosecute her claim; and she further declares that she has heretofore made *no* application for (16) *Bounty land but her pension pending claim No. 36.387.* _____ and that her residence is No. _____ _____ street, city (or town) of *Smithfield*, County of *Cache* State of *Utah*, and that her post office address is *the same*.

[Two attesting witnesses who can write their names.]

Hiram K Canny

Jas T Hammond

Caroline Harris
Signature of Claimant.

Caroline, in her old age, gave a description of her husband, Martin Harris, as she applied for a pension as his widow in 1879: "He was about five feet eight inches high, light complexioned with blue eyes."[95]

Mrs. Sariah Steel of Goshen, Utah, a grandchild of Caroline, stated that her grandmother, Caroline Harris, was never known by the name of Davis, either in the family circle or among neighbors or friends.

Louise Littlefield, a sister to Caroline, submitted the following affidavit: ". . . duly sworn July 24, 1879, that she had known the claiment, Caroline Harris and her deceased husband Martin Harris at Kirtland, Ohio, when they were married on or about November 1, 1837 [1836]. That the deceased always treated and acknowledged claiment as his lawful wife; and that they lived and cohabited together as such and were so received in society and were so regarded by their acquaintances, that she never heard the fact of their marriage disputed, that she often heard the deceased in his lifetime speak of the claimant as his wife. [96]

The following obituary was published in the *Logan Journal* and reprinted in the *Deseret News*.

On the 17th of Jan 1883, at the residence of her son, Martin, in Lewisville, Bingham Co., Idaho, Mrs. Caroline Harris, widow of the late Martin Harris, the well known witness of the Book of Mormon. She was the daughter of Patriarch John Young, deceased, and Theodocia Kimball. She was born in the town of Hector, Tompkins Co., N.Y. May 17, 1816. She died full in the belief of the everlasting Gospel and in hopes of a glorious resurrection. For several years past, her home was in Smithfield, but last fall she removed to Lewisville, intending to pass the winter with her son. For a year or more she has been a great sufferer. Her affliction was dropsy and heart disease. In addition to this, she had a paralytic stroke which seriously affected the limbs on the right side of her body, and even deprived her of the power of speech to the extent that for several months she was unable to articulate but a few words so as to be understood. Previous to her removal to Lewisville, she received much kindness from the people of Smithfield. Her funeral services and burial took place in Lewisville on the 19th inst.[97]

Mrs. Sariah Steele was seventeen years of age at the time of her grandmother's passing. She related that at the time of Caroline's death the temperature was forty degrees below zero. Mrs. Steele's father, Martin Harris, Jr., was the only one of Caroline's three sons present at the funeral. John was snow-bound in the lumber and railroad camp of Beaver Canyon on the Idaho-Montana border, and the whereabouts of Solomon was unknown at that time.[98]

Chapter V
Reconciled and Rewarded

When William H. Homer, a brother-in-law to Martin Harris, Jr., was eighty-one years of age, he wrote an account of his visit with Martin Harris in Kirtland, Ohio.

I first saw Martin Harris in Kirtland, Ohio, about the last of December, 1869. On my return from a mission to England, I stopped to visit some of my relatives in Pennsylvania. On resuming my journey, one of my cousins, James A. Crockett, who was not a member of the Church, came as far as Kirtland, Ohio, with me. We remained in Kirtland over night, and the next morning after breakfast we asked the landlord who was custodian of the Mormon Temple at Kirtland, and he informed us that Martin Harris was custodian and pointed out to us where we would find the old gentleman. Accordingly we went to the door and knocked. In answer to our knock there came to the door of the cottage a poorly clad, emaciated little man, on whom the winter of life was weighing heavily. It was Martin Harris. In his face might be read the story of his life. There were the marks of spiritual upliftment. There were the marks of keen disappointment. There was the hunger strain for the peace, the contentment, the divine calm that it seemed could come no more into his life. It was a pathetic figure, and yet it was a figure of strength. For with it all there was something about the little man which revealed the fact that he had lived richly; that into his life had entered such noble experiences as come to the lives of but few.

I introduced myself modestly as a brother-in-law of Martin Harris, Jr. — as he had married my eldest sister — and as an Elder of the Church who was returning from a foreign mission. The effect of the introduction was electric. But the fact of relationship was overwhelmed by the fact of Utah citizenship. The old man bristled with vindictiveness. "One of those Brighamite Mormons, are you?" he snapped. Then he railed impatiently against Utah and the founder of the Mormon commonwealth. It was in vain that I tried to turn the old man's attention to his family. Martin Harris was 86 years old at the time. Martin Harris seemed to be obsessed. He would not understand that there stood before him a man who knew his wife and children; who had followed the Church to Utah.

After some time, however, the old man said, "You want to see the temple, do you?" "Yes, indeed," I exclaimed, "if we may." "Well, I'll get the key," he answered. From that moment, Martin Harris, in spite of occasional outbursts, radiated with interest. He led us through the rooms of the temple and explained how they were used. He pointed out the place of the School of the Prophets. He showed where the temple curtain had at one time hung. He related thrilling experiences in connection with the history of the sacred building. In the basement, as elsewhere, there were many signs of delapidation; the plaster had fallen off the ceilings and the walls; windows were broken; the woodwork was stained and marred. Whether it was the influence of these conditions or not it is difficult to tell, but here again Martin Harris was moved to speak against the Utah Mormons. An injustice, a gross injustice had been done to him. He should have been chosen president of the Church.

When the old man was somewhat exhausted, I asked, "Is it not true that you were once very prominent in the Church; that you gave liberally of your means, that you were very active in the performance of your duties?" "That is very true," replied Martin. "Things were all right then. I was honored while the people were here, but now that I am old and poor it is all different. . . ."

74

"What about your testimony to the Book of Mormon? Do you still believe that the Book of Mormon is true and that Joseph Smith was a prophet?" Again the effect was electric. A changed old man stood before me. He was no longer a man with an imagined grievance. He was a man with a message.

"Young man," answered Martin Harris with impressiveness, "Do I believe it? Do I see the sun shining? Just as surely as the sun is shining on us and gives us light, and the moon and stars give us light by night, just as surely as the breath of life sustains us, so surely do I know that Joseph Smith was a true prophet of God, chosen of God to open the last dispensation of the fulness of times; so surely do I know that the Book of Mormon was divinely translated. I saw the plates; I saw the angel; I heard the voice of God. I know that the Book of Mormon is true and that Joseph Smith was a true Prophet of God. I might as well doubt my own existence as to doubt the divine authenticity of the Book of Mormon, or the divine calling of Joseph Smith."

It was a sublime moment. It was a wonderful testimony. We were thrilled to the very roots of our hair. The shabby, emaciated little man before us was transformed as he stood before us with hand outstreached toward the sun of heaven. A halo seemed to encircle him. A divine fire glowed in his eyes. His voice throbbed with sincerity and the conviction of his message. It was the real Martin Harris, whose burning testimony no power on earth could quench. It was the most thrilling moment of my life.

I asked Martin Harris how he could bear such a wonderful testimony after having left the Church. He said, "Young man, I never did leave the Church; the Church left me."

Martin Harris was now in a softer mood. He turned to me and asked, "Who are you?" I explained again our relationship. "So my son Martin married your sister," repeated the old man, shaking my hand. "You know my family then:" "Yes," I replied. "Wouldn't you like to see your family again?" "I should like to see Caroline and the children," mused Martin naming over the children, "But I cannot, I am too poor." "That need not stand in the way," I answered, "President Young would be only too glad to furnish means to convey you to Utah." "Don't talk Brigham Young," warned Martin, "he would not do anything that was right." "Send him a message by me," I persisted, now deeply concerned in the project. "No," declared Harris emphatically, "yet, I should like to see my family." "Then entrust me with a message," I pleaded. Martin paused. "Well," he said slowly, "I believe I will. You call on Brigham Young. Tell him about our visit. Tell him that Martin Harris is an old, old man, living on charity, with his relatives. Tell him I should like to visit Utah, my family and children — I would be glad to accept help from the Church, but I want no personal favor. Wait! Tell him that if he sends money, he must send enough for the round trip. I should not want to remain in Utah." For twenty-five [32] years he had nursed the old grudge against the leaders of the Church, probably because nobody had had the patience with him that I had shown.

After we had bidden Martin Harris good-bye, and had taken a few steps from the temple, my cousin placed his hands on my shoulders and said, "Wait a minute." Looking me squarely in the eyes, he said, "I can testify that the Book of Mormon is true. There is something within me that tells me that the old man told the truth. I know the Book of Mormon is true."

In due time I reached my home in the Seventh Ward in Salt Lake City. I recounted to my father my experiences with Martin Harris and we two set out immediately to report at the office of President

Young. The president received us very graciously. He listened attentively to my recital of my visit to Martin Harris. President Young asked questions now and again to make clear certain points. Then, when the story was told, he said, and it seemed to me that he beamed with pleasure, "I want to say this: I was never more gratified over any message in my life. Send for him? Yes! I shall send even if it were to take the last dollar of my own.

Martin Harris spent his time and money freely when one dollar was worth more than one thousand dollars are now. Send for him?

Yes, indeed I shall send. Rest assured Martin Harris will be here in time. It was Martin Harris who gave the Prophet Joseph Smith the first money to assist in the translation of the Book of Mormon. Martin Harris was the first scribe to assist in the translation of the Book of Mormon from the original plates, as dictated by the Prophet, who was led by the Holy Ghost. It was Martin Harris who was called, my revelation, to assist in the selection and ordination of the first council of the Twelve Apostles of the newly organized Church. It was Martin Harris who was called upon to accompany the Prophet to Missouri to assist in the selection of the land of consecration. Martin Harris also aided in the selection of the first High Council of the Church, and he was a member of said Council. When the new Presidency of the Church was chosen, Martin felt greatly disappointed that he was not called to leadership, but Martin Harris never denied the faith, never affiliated with any other sect or denomination, but when the Church came west Martin remained behind. It is true that Martin Harris did not apostatize; he was never tried for his fellowship; he was never excommunicated."[99]

Edward Stevenson, a member of the First Council of the Seventy, visited Martin Harris in 1870 at Kirtland, Ohio. He was instrumental in bringing Martin Harris to Utah. Mr. Stevenson wrote the following account:

While I was living in Michigan, then a Territory, in 1833, near the town of Pontiac, Oakland County, Martin Harris came there, and in a meeting, where I was present, bore testimony of the appearance of an angel exhibiting the golden plates, and commanding him to bear a testimony of these things to all people whenever opportunity was afforded him to do so; and I can say that his testimony had great effect in that vicinity. . . .

In the year 1869 I was appointed on a mission to The United States. [Upon completion of my mission] I visited New York and called to visit the sacred spot from where the plates of the Book of Mormon were taken, I found there an aged gentleman, 74 years old, who knew Martin Harris, and said that he was known in that neighborhood as an honest farmer, having owned a good farm three miles from that place. He further said that he well remembered the time when the 'Mormons' used to gather at Mormon Hill, as he termed it, where it was said the plates came from.

[Then] having visited several [other] of the Eastern States, I called at Kirtland, Ohio, to see the first Temple that was built by our people in this generation. While there, I again met Martin Harris, soon after coming out of the Temple. He took from under his arm a copy of the Book of Mormon, the first edition, I believe, and bore a faithful testimony, just the same as that I had heard him bear 36 years previous. He said that it was his duty to continue to lift up his voice as he had been commanded to do in defense of the book that he held in his hand, and offered to prove from the Bible that just such a book was to come forth out of the ground, and that, too, in a day when there were no Prophets on the earth, and that he was daily bearing testimony to many who visited the Temple. After patiently hearing him, I felt a degree of compassion for him, and in turn bore my testimony to him, as I had received it through obedience to the Gospel, and that the work was still [going] onward, and the words of Isaiah, 2nd chapter, that "the house of the Lord" was in the tops of the mountains, and that under the leadership of Pres. Young all nations were gathering to Zion to learn of God's ways and to walk in His paths. . . .

After my arrival in Utah in 1870, I was inspired to write to Martin Harris, and soon received a reply that the Spirit of God, for the first time prompted him to go to Utah. Several letters were afterwards exchanged. Pres. Brigham Young, having read the letters, . . . requested me to get a subscription and emigrate Martin to Utah, he subscribing $25 for that purpose. Having raised the subscription to about $200, I took the railroad cars for Ohio, July 19, 1870, and on the 10th of August, filled my appointment . . . finding Martin Harris elated with his prospective journey.

A very singular incident occurred at this time. While Martin was visiting his friends, bidding them farewell, his pathway crossed a large pasture, in which he became bewildered. Dizzy, faint and staggering through the blackberry vines that are so abundant in that vicinity, his clothes torn, bloody and faint, he lay down under a tree to die. After a time he revived, called on the Lord, and finally at 12 o'clock midnight, found his friend, and in his fearful condition was cared for and soon regained his strength. He related this incident as a snare of the adversary to hinder him from going to Salt Lake City. Although in his 88th year he possessed remarkable vigor and health, having recently worked in the garden, and dug potatoes by the day for some of his neighbors.

Aug. 19, 1870, in company with Martin Harris I left Kirtland for Utah, and on the 21st he was with me in Chicago, and at the American Hotel bore testimony to a large number of people of the visitation of the angel, etc. . . .[100]

On their way to Utah, Brother Stevenson and Martin Harris stayed in Des Moines, Iowa, and while they were there the Saints took up a collection and bought him a suit of clothes, which made "Martin feel like a new man."

After his arrival in Salt Lake City, Utah, the sisters of the Fifteenth Ward Relief Society offered to have a new set of artificial teeth made for him, to which he replied: "No, Sisters I thank you for your kindness, but I shall not live long. Take the money and give it to the poor."[101]

Brother Stevenson reported further:

> While on our journey I took occasion to teach Martin Harris the necessity of his being re-baptized. At first he did not seem to agree, . . . Finally he said, if it was right the Lord would manifest it to him by his spirit which He did. Soon after his arrival in Salt Lake City Martin came to my house and said the Spirit of the Lord had made it manifest to him, not only for himself personally, but also that he should be baptized for his dead, for he had seen his father seeking his aid. He saw his father at the foot of a ladder, striving to get up to him, and he went down to him taking him by the hand and helped him up. The baptismal font in the Endowment House was the place where I led Martin Harris down into the water and rebaptized him, 17 Sept. 1870. Five of the apostles were present . . . After baptism Orson Pratt confirmed him . . . after which he was baptized for some of his dead friends [relatives].[102]

In the same article, the *Millennial Star* printed the following: "Martin Harris arrived [with Elder Edward Stevenson] whose name is known almost throughout the world as one of the witnesses of the Book of Mormon. They left Kirtland on the 19th of August.

August 31st [1870], the Salt Lake *Herald* said:

> "Martin Harris, one of the three witnesses of the Book of Mormon, arrived in Salt Lake City last night, accompanied by Elder Edward Stevenson. Two members of the Des Moines Branch of the Church accompanied them to our city."

The *Deseret News* of August 31, 1870, in over one column, notices the arrival of Martin Harris last evening, at 7:30, "who is in his 88th year. He is remarkably vigorous for one of his years, his memory being very good, and his sight, though his eyes appear to have failed, being so acute that he can see to pick a pin off the ground. . . . He has never failed to bear testimony to the Divine authenticity of the Book of Mormon. He says it is not a matter of belief on his part, but of knowledge. He with the other two witnesses declared, and their testimony has accompanied every copy of the book, that 'an angel of God came down from heaven, and he brought and laid before our eyes, that we beheld and saw the plates, and the engravings thereon.' This declaration he had not varied from in 41 years. . . . We are glad to see Martin Harris once more in the midst of the Saints."

The Salt Lake *Herald*, September 3rd [1870]:

We had a call yesterday morning from Elder Edward Stevenson, who introduced Martin Harris, one of the "three witnesses" to the Book of Mormon. Mr. Harris is now 88 years of age, and is remarkably lively and energetic for his years. He holds firmly to the testimony he has borne for over forty years, that an angel appeared before him and the other witnesses, and showed them the plates upon which the characters of the Book of Mormon were inscribed. After living many years separated from the body of the Church, he has come to spend the evening of life among the believers in that book to which he is so prominent a witness. Mr. Harris, who has a number of relatives in the Territory, came from the East under the care of Elder Edward Stevenson.

Monday Evening News, September 5, 1870, contains the following:

SABBATH MEETINGS. — The congregation in the morning was addressed by Elder Edward Stevenson, Martin Harris and President George A. Smith. In the afternoon the time was occupied by Elder John Taylor, the house was crowded to overflowing.

Martin Harris related an incident that occurred during the time that he wrote that portion of the translation of the Book of Mormon which he was favored to write direct from the mouth of the Prophet Joseph Smith. He said that the Prophet possessed a seer stone, by which he was enabled to translate as well as from the Urim and Thummim, and for convenience he then used the seer tone. Martin explained the translation as follows: By aid of the seer stone, sentences would appear and were read by the Prophet and written by Martin, and when finished he would say, 'Written,' and if correctly written, that sentence would disappear and another appear in its place, but if not written correctly it remained until corrected, so that the translation was just as it was engraven on the plates, precisely in the language then used. Martin said, after continued translation they would become weary, and would to down to the river and exercise by throwing stones out on the river, etc. While so doing on one occasion, Martin found a stone very much resembling the one used for translation, and on resuming their labor of translation, Martin put in place the stone that he had found. He said that the Prophet remained silent, unusally and intently gazing in darkness, no traces of the usual sentences appearing. Much surprised, Joseph exclaimed, 'Martin! What is the matter? All is as dark as Egypt!' Martin's countenance betrayed him, and the Prophet asked Martin why he had done so. Martin said, 'to stop the mouths of fools,' who had told him that the Prophet had learned those sentences and was merely repeating them, etc.

Martin said further that the seer stone differed in apperance entirely from the Urim and Thummim that was obtained with the plates, which were two clear stones set in two rims, very much resembling spectacles, only they were larger. Martin said there were not many pages (116) translated while he wrote, after which Oliver Cowdery and others did the writing.

. . . Brother Harris was taught the necessity of being rebaptized. He said that was new doctrine to him. Revelations, 2nd chapter, was explained, that those who had lost their first love and had fallen into evils and snares, were called on to "repent and do their first works," and that rebaptism was a part of the Gospel. He claimed that he had not been cut off from the Church, but said if that was required of him it would be manifested to him by the Spirit. Soon after his arrival in Utah he applied for baptism, saying that the Spirit had made known to him that it was his duty to renew his covenant before the Lord.

He was also taught a principle that was new to him — baptism for the dead, as taught and practiced by the ancient Saints, and especially taught by Paul the Apostle in the 15th chapter of 1st Corinthians: "Else what shall they do which are baptized for the dead, if the dead rise not at all? Why are they then baptized for the dead." After consideration he came and said it had been made known to him that baptism for the dead was a correct principle, for he had seen his father in vision at the foot of a ladder, and he was above, and had to go down and help him up. In a short time the baptismal font was prepared, and by his request I baptized him, and President Geo. A. Smith, and Apostles John Taylor, Wilford Woodruff, Jos. F. Smith and Orson Pratt confirmed him by the laying on of hands, Orson Pratt being mouth. As soon as he was confirmed he returned to the font and was baptized for several of his dead friends — father, grandfathers, etc.

Then his sister also was baptized for the female relatives, and they were confirmed for and in behalf of those who they were baptized for, by the same brethren, Jos. F. Smith being mouth. It was a time of rejoicing for all who were present.

Brother Martin visited many of the wards, continuing to bear his testimony both of what he had beheld with his own eyes, and verily knew to be true. He publicly said that many years ago, in Ohio, a number of persons combined and sought to get Martin to drink wine for the purpose of crossing him in his testimony. At the conclusion they asked him if he really believed the testimony that he had signed in the Book of Mormon to be true? He replied no, he did not believe it, but, much to their surprise, he said he *knew* it to be true.[103]

The *Journal History* (June 1, 1877) contains the following items:

The immense Tabernacle and the Temple . . . and in fact the beautiful city in full view . . . looked wonderful to Brother Harris who seemed wrapped in admiration and exclaimed, "who would have thought that the Book of Mormon would have done all this?"[104]

His abiding testimony and his assistance with his property to publish the Book of Mormon have earned a name for him that will endure while time shall last.[105]

Salt Lake City, September 4, 1970, Sunday Morning: Testimony of Martin Harris, written by my hand (Edward Stevenson) from the mouth of Martin Harris:

In the year 1818, fifty-two years ago I was inspired of the Lord and taught of the spirit that I should not join any church, although I was anxiously sought for by many of the secterians. I was taught I could not walk together unless agreed. What can you not be agreed in? In the trinity, because I cannot find it in any Bible. Find it for me and I am ready to receive it. Three persons in one God — one personage I can not concede to, for this is anti-Christ . . . Other sects also tried me. They say three persons in one God, without body, parts or passions. I told them such a God I would not be afraid of. I could not please or offend him. (I) would not be able to fight a duel with such a God . . . All of the sects called me "Bro" (Brother) because the Lord had enlightened me. The spirit told me to join none of the churches, for none had authority from the Lord, for there will not be a true church on the earth until the words of Isaiah shall be fulfilled . . . for the spirit told me that I might just as well plunge myself into the water as to have anyone of the sects baptize me. So I remained until the Church was organized by Joseph Smith, the Prophet. Then I was baptized by the hands of Oliver Cowdery, by Joseph Smith's command, being the first after Joseph and Oliver Cowdery. And then the spirit bore testimony that this was all right, and I rejoiced in the established Church. Previous to my being baptized, I became a witness of the plates of the Book of Mormon in 1829. In March the people rose up and united against the work, gathering testimony against the plates, and said they had testimony enough, and if I did not put Joseph in jail and his father for deception, they would me.[105]

Sunday Oct. 9, 1870 General Conference, morning session . . . Mr. Martin Harris, one of the three witnesss to the Book of Mormon, arose and bore testimony of its divine authenticity.[106] Thus fulfilling the commandment given him, (D&C 19:20) "Publish it upon the mountains and upon every high place, and among every people that thou art permitted to see.

In the Social Hall in Salt Lake City, a party was held October 10, 1870, for the survivors of Zion's camp and the Mormon Battalion. Martin Harris was honored as one.[107]

The next day, October 11, 1870, he went to the Endowment House to participate in the sacred ordinances performed there. While Martin was staying with his grandniece, Irinda Crandall McEwan, he was visited by his former wife, Caroline (Young) Harris Davis, who lived nearby.[108]

The manuscript of William Pilkington gives an interesting bit of information reflecting Martin's family relationships: After staying a few days in Salt Lake City and Ogden he went to live in Smithfield, Cache County, Utah, where his wife and family lived. Here he resided until 1874.

The aged witness often reminisced, revealing some of his early spiritual experiences and disappointments to young Willie Pilkington. Of these times Pilkington wrote:

> It was no longer a man with an Imagined grievence. It was a man with a message, a man with noble Convictions in his Heart. Inspired of God and endowed with a Divine Knowledge He said, Just as sure as You see the Sunshining. Just as sure am I that I stood in The presence of an Angel of God, with Joseph Smith and saw him hold the Gold Plates in his Hands. I also saw the Urim and Thummin, The Breastplate and the Sword of Laban I saw the Angel descend from Heaven. The Heavens were then opened and I heard the voice of God declare, that every thing the Angel had told us was True, and that the Book of Mormon was Translated correct. I was commanded by God's Voice to testify to the whole world what I had seen and heard."
>
> In his talks with me he would say, he had asked me many times if I would tell the people what he had told me and he repeated, "Now, Willie, you won't forget to tell the people what I have told you, will you, after I am dead and gone?" And he would hold up his hand to the square and say that he was telling the truth. And I would tell him, "No, Grandpa, I won't; I will sure tell the people what you have told me, for I know that you have told me the truth."[109]

Another report states: "He, Martin, is remarkably vigorous . . . his memory very good. . . . He has never failed to bear testimony to the divine authenticity of the Book of Mormon. He says 'it is not a matter of belief on my part, but knowledge . . . that an angel of God came down from Heaven, and brought and laid before our eyes, that we beheld and saw the plates and the engravings thereon! This declaration he has not varied from, in forty-one years."[110]

In Cache County, where Martin lived until his death at Clarkston, he continued, as was his custom, to bear his testimony. Shortly before his death he related the following to Ole A. Jensen:

> I will tell you a wonderful thing that happened. After Joseph had found the plates, three of us took some tools to go to the hill (Cumorah) and hunt for some more boxes of gold or something and indeed we found a stone box.
>
> We got quite excited, but dug quite carefully around it and (when) we were ready to take it up, but behold by some unseen power slid it slipped back into the hill. We stood there looked at it and one of us took a crowbar and tried to drive it through the lid to hold it but it glanced (off) and broke one corner off the box. Some time that box will be found and you will find one corner broken off the box and then you will know that I have told the truth. Brother, as sure as you are standing there and see me, just so, we did see the Angel and the Golden Plates in his hands and he showed them to me. I have promised that I will bear witness of this truth both here and hereafter.[111]

Many accounts of Martin Harris' testimony exist, varying very little in content, confirming his renewed testimony of the divine calling of Joseph Smith coupled with his unwavering testimony of the *Book of Mormon*. At one time Martin expressed his conviction of the visitation of angels, as he had seen and talked with them and observed their bodily forms.

William (Willie) Pilkington, who with him, shared the home of Martin Harris, Jr., for two years, heard repeatedly the events in the life of the third witness and recorded: "He said that the people said he had apostatized, but not so, nor was he ever officially excommunicated . . . He remained separated from the Church, he was like a sheep without a shepherd, outside the flock, but . . . and he would hold up his hand to the square and say he was telling the truth.[112]

A F F I D A V I T

STATE OF UTAH.   )
) SS
COUNTY OF BOX ELDER.)

                    I, George Godfrey, being first duly sworn, do depose and say:-

           During the life of Martin Harris, one of the three witnesses to the Book of Mormon, I had ample opportunity to become well acquainted with the said Martin Harris, having met him the first time at Salt Lake City, Utah, near the year 1867, as my memory serves me, and at that time considered it a privilege to shake hands with a man who had had the experiences and the testimony which he bore witness to. Later he moved to Smithfield, Cache County, Utah, and later moved to Clarkston, same county where he died in the year 1875. Prior to his death and in his last sickness I sat up nights with him upon many an occasion, in connection with my Brothers, John E. Godfrey and Thomas Godfrey, both of whom now reside at Clarkston, aforesaid, and who can make affidavit to the things I am herein stating; that many times I have heard the said Martin Harris bear witness to the truthfulness and genuineness of the Book of Mormon, at times when he was enjoying good health and spirits and when he was on his deathbed; that his testimony never varied; that I have seen others and that I myself have tried to entrap him relative to the testimony which he bore, by cros questioning him relative to the scenes and events which are Church History in connection with the bringing forth of the Book of Mormon; that upon all of these questions his mind was clear as it is possible for the human mind to be, and that his testimonies have left no tract of doubt in my mind that he actually conversed with an angel who bore testimony to him of the truthfulness of the records contained in the Book of Mormon; that he saw and handled the gold plates from which the said records were taken; that a few hours before his death, and when he was so weak and enfeebled that he was unable to recognize me or anyone, and knew not to whom he was speaking, I asked him if he did not feel that there was an element, at least, of fraudulence and deception in the things that were written and told of the coming forth of the Book of Mormon, and he replied as he had always done, and many, many times in my hearing, and with the same spirit that he always manifested when enjoying health and vigor: "The Book of Mormon is no fake. I know what I know. I have seen what I have seen, and I have heard what I have heard. I have seen and handled the gold plates from which the Book of Mormon is written,. An angel appeared to me and others and testified to the truthfulness of the record, and had I been willing to have perjured myself and sworn falsely to the testimony I now bear, I could have been a rich man, but I could not have testified other than I have done and am now doing, for these things are true." That I prepared the grave and assisted in the burial of the said Martin Harris in the Clarkston graveyard, where the remains now rest.

                                              GEORGE GODFREY
                                    _____

Subscribed and sworn to before me this 29th day of October, 1921.

                                    JOHN J. SHUMWAY
                                      Notary Public
                                    Residing at Garland, Utah

My commission expires May 11, 1925.

COPY

One of Martin's numerous testimonies.

Original held by:
Ezra Harris
Tremonton, Utah

Another lasting memory was recorded by Joseph Homer Snow (2nd son of James C. Snow and Jane Cecelia Roberts). He told of special events during his early life in Cache County, Utah. One of them was when Martin Harris had dinner with his family. He remembered well how they were all washed and combed in preparation. This is the way he recorded the event:

> When I was a small boy of about six years, mother said to us children, "There'll be one of the witnesses to the Book of Mormon to take some dinner with us. I'm going to ask him some questions, and I want you children to pay strict attention to what he says."
>
> So, when he came to dinner, mother asked him these questions: "Did you actually see an angel and hear him speak?"
>
> He said, "Just as much so as I see you and hear you speak. And I also know that the others heard him speak."
>
> "Will you describe how he stood?" Mother asked.
>
> He said, "He stood at least twenty inches off the ground, and he had records in his hand — The Book of Mormon. He turned the leaves and declared that it was the work of the Lord and that it was true. He commanded us to bear that testimony to the world."[113]

The dying testimony of Martin Harris has been recorded by William Pilkington:

> On the 9th day of July, 2879, while he was dying, I knelt by his cot, I wanted to get what I thought would be his last words, but he could not talk audible. I could not understand what he wanted to tell me . . . so I stroked his hair back on his forehead and knelt down and prayed to the Lord and asked him in the name of Jesus to strengthen his servant's voice so that I could understand his last words, but I could get no response. He was lying on his left side,

facing in the room, and as I knelt down I placed my hands on his right arm, and as I moved to stand up . . . he shook his head, as if he did not want me to move. I then knelt down again and prayed to the Lord as before and I was inspired by the Lord to ask Grandpa if he wanted me to hold up his right hand so that he could bare (sic) his testimony. I asked him and his answer came clear, yes! While I held his right hand up strength was given to him and he bore his testimony, as he had done many times before, and I understood every word. He then bore the same testimony to the whole world, and then lay back exhausted. There were two other men standing in the room and heard him bare [sic] his testimony.[114]

Noble experiences had come into his life, such as come into the lives of very few men. Elder William Harrison Homer, Jr., a neighbor, has written concerning this time:

The next day July 10, 1875 marked the end. . . . I stood by the bedside holding the patient' right hand . . . Martin Harris had been unconscious for a number of days. When we first entered the room the old gentleman seemed to be sleeping. He soon woke up and asked for a drink of water. I put my arms under the old gentleman, raised him . . . He drank freely, then, said, "Yes, I did see the plates on which the Book of Mormon was written; I did see the angel; I did hear the voice of God; and I do know that Joseph Smith is a Prophet of God, holding the keys of the Holy Priesthood." This was the end. Martin Harris, divinely chosen witness of the work of God relaxed, gave up my hand. He lay back on his pillow and just as the sun went down behind the Clarkston mountains, the spirit of Martin Harris passed on.[115]

When Martin Harris, Jr., reported his father's death and burial to the First Presidency of the Church, he told that his father was buried with his Book of Mormon in his right hand and the Doctrine and Covenants in his left.[116]

His reconciliation with the Church had been properly effected through President Brigham Young, and now this great benefactor of the sacred Book of Mormon record had gone to his reward as promised through Joseph Smith, Sr., the Patriarch:

Thou shalt stand upon the earth when the kingdom of this world shall end, and the kingdom of heaven come down, if thou art faithful . . . thou shalt know Christ more perfectly, for thou shalt see him and converse with him face to face. Thy mind shall be enlarged, and thy testimony shall yet convince its thousands and its tens of thousands; yea it shall shine like the sun, and though the wicked seek to overthrow it, it shall be in vain, for the Lord God shall bear it off victorious. The holy angels will watch over thee and bear thee up in their hands.[117]

EPILOGUE

The fiftieth anniversary of the death of Martin Harris was commemorated by the dedication of a monument in Clarkston, Utah, to his memory. President Heber J. Grant spoke at the services and dedicated the monument. A record of that day's events was published in several newspapers and is here given:

> On Friday, July 10, 1925, a large concourse of people, nearly one thousand, from different parts of Cache County gathered at Clarkston to honor the memory of Martin Harris, one of the three men who was shown by an angel the plates from which the Book of Mormon was translated. The day, also, was the 50th anniversary of the death of Martin Harris.

> The services were under the direction of the Benson Stake Presidency, Elder John E. Griffin, 2nd Counselor conducting the program. The opening song, "We Thank Thee Oh God for a Prophet," was sung by the entire assembly. A prayer was offered by Bishop John Ravsten. A mixed quartette sang "An Angel from On High," and a short account of the life of Martin Harris was given.

> The monument was unveiled by Russel Harris, a son of Martin Harris, Junior. . . . The monument is a beautiful polished granite shaft; and stands a little more than 18 ft. in height. The shaft is 2 ft. 2 in. square at the base and tapers to a point, being 12 ft. high. The dye is 2 ft. 1 in. square at the base and 3 ft. high. On this dye is beautifully inscribed as follows:

> > "Martin Harris one of the three witnesses to the Divine Authenticity of the Book of Mormon. Born Easton, Saratoga County, New York, May 18, 1783. Died Clarkston, Utah, July 10, 1875."[119]

From the writing of William H. Homer, Jr., we find this challenge given at a family reunion:[120]

To the living descendants of Russell King Homer, may I suggest that when we visit our ancestral home in Clarkston, Utah, as many of us often do, and go to the cemetery to pay our respects to our cherished ancestor, and perhaps lay a wreath upon his grave, let us also ever remember the esteem in which we hold the name of Martin Harris, that chosen one of God. As we stand beside that consecrated ground which marks his mortal resting place, may we bow our heads in humble reverence to his memory. And may our souls rejoice in the knowledge that Martin Harris was in the end privileged to answer that divine plea of the Master, when he said unto Martin, "Yea, come unto me, thy Savior. Amen."[119] (Wm. H. Homer, Jr., ch. VII)

CHRONOLOGY OF THE LIFE OF MARTIN HARRIS

1783   May 18, born in Easton, Washington County (now Saratoga), New York.

1790   In census with parents, Nathan and Rhoda Lapham Harris, in Washington County, New York.

1793   Moved with parents to Palmyra, Ontario (now Wayne), New York.

1794   Father bought 600 acres in Palmyra for fifty cents an acre.

1808   March 27, married his cousin, Lucy Harris, daughter of Rufus and Lucy Harris. Martin, age twenty-five years; Lucy, almost sixteen years.

1810   In census in Palmyra, New York, age between twenty-six-forty-five years; wife between sixteen-twenty-six; female child under ten years; another female between sixteen-twenty-six.

1812   In War of 1812.

1824   Built farm house.

1825   Hired Joseph Smith, Sr., and Hyrum to work for him, rocking up a well. Heard of "vision".

Deeded eighty acres to wife through her brother, Peter Harris.

1827   Fall, Martin gave Joseph Smith fifty dollars to help him to move 155 miles to Harmony, Pennsylvania, to commence translation of the plates.

1828   February 29, Martin followed Joseph to Harmony. At Joseph's request, Martin took copies of the Egyptian characters and their translation to New York City to see Professor Anton. Martin drove his team. Returned to Palmyra by way of Harmony, Pennsylvania. Rented farm.

1828   April 12, Martin went to Harmony to serve as scribe for Joseph in translation of 116 pages. Finished June 14, 1828.

1828   June 14, Martin brought manuscript back to Palmyra to show his parents; his brother, Preserved; his wife, Lucy, and her sister, Mrs. Freeman Cobb (Polly Harris). By showing others, he lost 116 pages.

1828   July, chastized by the Lord (D&C 3:12). Discord continued between Martin and Lucy. Their oldest daughter, Lucy, courted by Mr. Dykes.

1828   August, Martin appeared in court in Lyons, New York (near Palmyra), as witness for Joseph Smith, Jr., Martin stated Joseph did not defraud him.

1829   June, Martin went to Fayette, Seneca, New York, (one day's travel). Desired to become a witness to the Book of Mormon. Martin returned to Palmyra.

1829   July 1, translation completed in 75 working days with Oliver Cowdery as scribe.

        Martin accompanied Joseph's parents to Whitmer home. Became witness to Book of Mormon.

1829   August, Martin mortgaged farm for $3,000 for 5,000 copies of the Book of Mormon. Printing began August, 1829.

1830   March 30, printing completed, seven months work. Martin sold 150 acres of land and his home for $3,000 in gold to pay the mortgage.

1830   April 6, Church organized at the home of Peter Whitmer, Sr., Fayette, Seneca, New York.

       April 6, Martin Harris baptized by Oliver Cowdery under direction of Joseph Smith, along with Porter Rockwell and Prophet's parents.

1830   June 9, Martin ordained a priest at Church conference at Fayette, New York, along with Joseph Smith, Sr., and Hyrum Smith.

       Martin and Lucy separated.

1831   May 27, Martin led about 50 Church members from Palmyra, headed for Kirtland, Ohio. They went through Buffalo, New York, by way of Erie Canal. Arrived June, 1831.

1831   June 6, ordained high priest at Kirtland conference under hands of Lyman Wight.

1831   Summer, accompanied Prophet to Missouri to establish Zion. Present at dedication of temple site at Independence, Missouri, August 3.

       Martin called to be first to observe law of consecration.

1831   Chosen to supervise Church publications.

1832   Martin and brother, Emer, raised up a branch of the Church in Springville, Susquehanny, Pennsylvania, with 70 members. Letter dated December 24 said: "Emer and Martin baptized 100 persons at Chenango Point (now known as Binghamton) New York, within a few weeks, signed, Newel."

1834   January, returned to Kirtland.

1834   Martin chosen a member of first High Council.

1834   Volunteered to go to Jackson County, Missouri, to relieve Saints. Left Kirtland April 1 as member of Zion's Camp. June 16, had experience with snake. Rebuked by Prophet.

1835   February 14, Martin blessed with Oliver Cowdery and David Whitmer to select and set apart the Twelve Apostles. The Three Witnesses were blessed under the hands of Joseph Smith, Jr., Sydney Rigdon, and Frederick G. Williams.

1835   August 27, patriarchal blessing from Joseph Smith, Sr.

1835   November 18, attended the funeral of his father, Nathan Harris, at the home of his brother, Preserved Harris, in Mentor, Ohio. Sermon preached by Joseph Smith, Jr.

1836   1836   Summer, wife, Lucy Harris, age 44, died.

1836   November 1, Martin married Caroline Young (niece of Brigham Young), in Kirtland, Ohio.

1837   September 3, dropped from high council.

1838   January 28, a son, Martin Harris, Jr., born in Kirtland, Geauga County, Ohio.

1840   Daughter born and died before 1850.

1842   April 29, a daughter, Julia Lacothia Harris, born in Kirtland, Lake County, Ohio.

1842   November 7, Martin rebaptized.

Remained in Kirtland while Saints went through persecution in Missouri and Nauvoo.

1844   June 27, Prophet martyred at Carthage, Illinois.

1845   July 11, a son, John Wheeler Harris, born in Kirtland, Lake County, Ohio.

1846   Fall, Martin Harris went to England to serve a mission with the Strangites. He continued to bear testimony of the divine origin of the Book of Mormon.

1850   Martin in Lake County, Ohio, census with wife, Caroline, and above named children. Also, one-year old Sarah Harris.

1854   December 1, Solomon Webster Harris, a son, born in Kirtland, Lake County, Ohio.

1854   Martin self-appointed guide at the Kirtland Temple.

1856   Spring, Caroline left from Kirtland to join Saints and her family in Utah. Gave birth to daughter, Ida May Harris, born May 27 in Iowa. Arrived in Utah fall of 1859 with five children; fate of daughter Sarah unknown.

1860   Martin in census of Kirtland, Lake County, Ohio, with son George, age 47, and George's wife, Mary Harris, age 20. This is George's second wife, Mary J. Thompson, whom he had married December 28, 1858, in Kirtland. Martin's occupation stated as "Mormon Preacher."

1870   Martin listed in census, age 88, in household of Joseph Hollisten, age 88, and wife, Electa, age 66. Martin contacted by Utah Saints and invited to come to Utah. Came with Edward Stevenson by train. Stopped in Des Moines, Iowa. Bore testimony to Saints there, who took up a collection to buy him a new suit.

1870   August 30, arrived in Salt Lake City, Utah.

1870   September 17, rebaptized in Endowment House font by Edward Stevenson, and confirmed by Elder Orson Pratt. Baptism witnessed by George A. Smith, John Taylor, Wilford Woodruff, and Joseph F. Smith.

Martin and his sister, Naomi Harris (Kellogg) Bent were baptized for their deceased relatives.

1870   October 10, a party was held in Salt Lake for the survivors of Zion's Camp and the Mormon Battalion. It was held in the Social Hall. Martin was one of the survivors of Zion's Camp.

Martin went to Smithfield to live with his son Martin Harris, Jr. Caroline, former wife, also resided in Smithfield, Cache County, Utah.

1874   Moved to Clarkston, Utah, with son, Martin and his family.

1875 July 10, Martin died after again bearing his testimony.

CHRONOLOGY OF THE LIFE OF CAROLINE YOUNG HARRIS

1816   May 17, born at Hector, Schuyler County, New York, daughter of John and Theodocia Kimball Young.

       Moved to Kirtland, Ohio, with parents.

1836   November 1, married Martin Harris. Ceremony performed by Heber C. Kimball.

1838   January 28, gave birth to son, Martin Harris, Jr., born in Kirtland, Geauga (now Lake) County, Ohio.

1840   Daughter born (died before 1850 census).

1842   April 29, gave birth to daughter, Julia Lacothia Harris.

1845   July 11, gave birth to son, John Wheeler.

1846   January 7, Caroline baptized (could be a rebaptism).

1846   Fall, husband, Martin, went to England on mission with Strangites.

1849   Gave birth to daughter, Sarah (age one-year in Kirtland, Lake County, Ohio, 1850 census).

1850   Appeared in Lake County, Ohio, census, with Martin and above-named children.

1854   December 1, gave birth to son, Soloman Webster, born in Kirtland, Lake County, Ohio, as were all the above-named children.

1856   Arrived at Church headquarters in Iowa.

1856   May 27, gave birth to daughter, Ida May Harris, probably in Pottawattamie County. Remained in Iowa three years.

1859   September 1, Caroline and five children arrived in Salt Lake City, Utah, with Captain Haight's oxen wagon train.

1860   January 16, married John Catley Davis.

1860   March 1, sealed in Endowment House to Mr. Davis at same time as daughter, Julia, was married and sealed to Davis' son, Elijah W. Davis.

1860   November 19, gave birth to a son, Joseph Harris Davis, at Payson, Utah. He died November 21.

1867   Family lived in Seventeenth Ward, Salt Lake City, Utah.

1867   August 28, Caroline had Emer Harris, Harriet H. Daley, and Martin Henderson Harris stay overnight in her home in Salt Lake. They had come to do temple work in the Endowment House.

Caroline separated from Davis and resumed the name of Caroline Harris. She moved to Smithfield, Cache County, Utah, to be near her eldest son, Martin, Jr.

1870   August 30, Martin, Sr., arrived in Utah. He went to Smithfield to live.

1887   Fall, went to Lewisville, Bingham County, Idaho, to visit son, Martin, Jr.

1888   January 17, died at home of son, Martin, Jr. Buried in Lewisville, Idaho on January 19.

FOOTNOTES

Martin Harris

[1]*Palmyra Courier* — Old Newspaper #22, p. 3. Photocopy in possession of the authors.

[1A]Willard Bean, A.B.O. *History of Palmyra* (Palmyra, N.Y.:Palmyra Courier Co., Inc. 1938); p. 14.

[2]Thomas L. Cook, *Palmyra and Vicinity* (Palmyra, N.Y. 1930), p. 204.

[3]*Palmyra Courier* — Old Newspapers, p. 2, 3.

[4]Orsamus G. Turner, *Phelps and Gorham's Purchase* (Rochester, N.Y.: W. Alling, 1851), p. 385.

[5]*Palmyra Courier* — Old Newspaper #23, p. 1. Photocopy in possession of the authors.

[6]Martin Harris — application for pension, 1860. In possession of Belle H. Wilson.

[7]Early Ontario Court Records, Lyons, New York. Book D, p. 191.

[8]Journal History, June 1, 1877, pp. 1-2; Historical Department, The Church of Jesus Christ of Latter-day Saints.

[9]Martin Harris — application for pension, 1860. Photocopy in possession of the authors.

[10]Orsamus G. Turner, Phelps and Gorham's Purchase. Rochester, New York: A Alling, 1851, p. 385.

[11]Willard Bean, p. 35.

[12]Smith, Lucy Mack, *History of Joseph Smith*, edited by Preston Nibley (Salt Lake City, Utah: Stevens and Wallis, 1945) pp. 114-115.

[13]Early Ontario Court Records, Lyons, New York, Book H. pp. 531–32.

[14]Lucy Mack Smith, p. 114.

[15]Lucy Mack Smith, p. 115.

[16]Joseph Smith, *History of The Church*, Vol. I, p. 21.

[17]Lucy Mack Smith, p. 116.

[18]Lucy Mack Smith, p. 116.

[19]Lucy Mack Smith, p. 117.

[20]Lucy Mack Smith, p. 117.

[21]Lucy Mack Smith, pp. 117-118.

[22]Pomroy Tucker, *Origin and Rise and Progress of Mormonism*, (Palmyra, N.Y.: D. Appleton and Co., 1867), pp. 443–45; see Rhett S. James, Bibliography.

[23]*Ensign*, July 1980, p. 71, and inside front and back covers.

[24]*Ensign*, July 1980, pp. 69-73.

[25]Lucy Mack Smith, pp. 121–122.

[26]Joseph Smith, Jr., Vol. I, pp. 20–21.

[27]T.W.P. Taylder, The Mormon's Own Book, 1855; in Special Collections, Harold B. Lee Library, Brigham Young University.

[28]Edward Stevensen, "One of the Three Witnesses, *Deseret News*, Dec. 13, 1881.

[29]Joseph Smith, Jr., Vol. I, p. 21.

[30]William Pilkington, Jr., *Autobiography*, 1938, p. 11; Historical Department, The Church of Jesus Christ of Latter-day Saints.

[31]T.W.P. Taylder, p. 23.

[32]T.W.P. Taylder, p. 24.

[33]"The Last Testimony of Sister Emma," *The Saints Herald*; Plano, Ill., Oct. 1, 1879. Contributed by Larry C. Porter.

[34]William Pilkington, Jr., p. 11.

35Lucy Mack Smith, pp. 130-131.

36Pomroy Tucker, p. 20.

37Pomroy Tucker, p. 45.

38Willard Bean, p. 51.

39Pomroy Tucker, p. 46.

40Lucy Mack Smith, p. 132.

41Lucy Mack Smith, pp. 128–129.

42*Palmyra Courier* — Old Newspaper, May 2, 1872, p. 4.

43Lucy Mack Smith, pp. 154–155.

44Willard Bean, p. 57.

45Joseph Smith, Jr., Vol. I, pp. 54–57.

46Joseph Smith, Jr., Vol. I, pp. 57.

47Willard Bean, p. 57.

48Brigham H. Roberts, *A Comprehensive History of the Church of Jesus Christ of Latter-day Saints* (Salt Lake City, Utah: Book Craft, 1968), vol. I, pp. 142–143.

49David Buel Dille, Manuscript, Sep. 15, 1853, *Millennial Star*, Vol. 21, page 545, The Church of Jesus Christ of Latter-day Saints.

50Thomas Gregg, cited by Rhett S. James, *The Prophet of Palmyra*. (New York: John B. Alden, 1890), pp. 36, 37, 38. In Special Collections, B.Y.U.

51Thomas Gregg, pp. 36, 37. 39.

52Wayne County Records, Deed Book, H325, Lyons, New York, Aug. 25, 1829.

53*Palmyra Courier* — Old Newspaper #25, p. 2, May 31, 1872. Photo copy in possession of the authors.

54*Palmyra Courier*, p. 2.

55Pomroy Tucker, p. 61, cited by Rhett S. James (see bibliography).

[56]Larry Porter, ",the Joseph Knight Family", *Ensign*, Oct. 1978, p. 40; original spelling and punctuation.

[57]Edward Stevensen Private Journal XXXII, Salt Lake City, Sept. 4, 1870, a letter.

[58]Larry Porter, "The Joseph Knight Family", *Ensign*, Oct. 1978, p. 40.

[59]Wayne County Records, Book H526, Apr. 7, 1831, Martin Harris to Thomas Lakey; also, Cook, *Plmyra and Vicinity*, p. 206.

[60]Robert Fresh, president of The Cobblestone Society and head curator of the Rochester Museum, Lecture, Jan. 20, 1977.

[61]*Palmyra Courier Journal*, Palmyra, New York, 1930; also *The Contributor*, Aug. 1844, vol. 406.

[62]Journal History, Feb. 22, 1831, p. 1–2.

[63]News Item in *Wayne Sentinel*, (Palmyra, New York: Palmyra Free Press, May 27, 1831.)

[64]Stanley B. Kimball, "The First Road West," *Ensign*, Jan. 1979, p. 30.

[65]Joseph Smith, Jr., vol. I, p. 188.

[66]Joseph Smith, Jr., vol I; footnote on p. 236.

[67]Extract of letters from the Elders Abroad, William W. Phelps, *Evening and Morning Star*, vol. I, #9, Independence, Missouri, Feb. 1836, p. 139.

[68]Franklin S. Harris, Sr., in Special Collections, Harold B. Lee Library, Brigham Young University, Provo, Utah; original spelling and punctuation retained in letters from Emer Harris.

[69]Joseph Smith, Jr., vol. II, p. 95.

[70]Joseph Smith, Jr., vol. II, pp.186-187.

[71]Isaac Decker, Document, Sept. 21, 1870, cited by Gunnell, Historical Department, The Church of Jesus Christ of Latter-day Saints.

[72]Hyrum L. and Helen Mae Andrus, *They Knew The Prophet* (Salt Lake City: Bookcraft, Inc., 1974) pp.22–23.

[73]Joseph Smith, Sr., to Martin Harris, Patriarchal Blessing, Aug. 27, 1835, vol. II, Historical Department, The Church of Jesus Christ of Latter-day Saints.

[74]Heber C. Kimball and extracts from the Journal of Elder Heber C. Kimball, *Times and Seasons*, Nauvoo, Illinois, filed in vol. VI. no. 1, p. 771.

[75]N.B. Lundwall, compiler, *Temples of the Most High*, (Salt Lake City: Zion's Printing and Publishing Co., Feb. 26, 1941), p. 41.

[76]B.H. Roberts, *Comprehensive History of the Church*, vol. I, p. 402.

[77]*Millennial Star*, vol. 25, p. 518, Aug. 8, 1863.

[78]Joseph Smith, Jr., vol. II, p. 510.

[79]Journal History, June 1, 1877, pp.1–2.

[80]William H. Homer, Jr., "The Passing of Martin Harris," *Improvement Era*, p. 471.

[81]Introduction to Church History, Nov. 7, 1842.

[82]Journal History, June 1, 1877, pp.1–2.

[83]Journal History, June 1, 1877, pp.1–2.

[84]Introduction to Church History, Historical Department, May 23, 1841.

[85]Richard Lloyd Anderson, *Investigating the Book of Mormon* (Salt Lake City: Deseret Book Co., 1981), quoting a letter of George Mantle to Marietta Walker, Dec. 26, 1888.

[86]Journal History, June 1, 1877, pp.1–2.

[87]David Buel Dille, Manuscript, Spring 1853, Historical Department, The Church of Jesus Christ of Latter-day Saints.

[88]Journal History, June 1, 1877, pp.1–2.

[89]Gunnell, *Martin Harris, Witness and Benefactor*, unpublished thesis, BYU, 1955, pp.124–125.

[90]*Homespun, Lydia Knight's History*, Noble Women's Lives Series (Salt Lake City: Juvenile Instructor Office, 1883), pp. 98–99.

[91]Endowment House Marriage Record, under date.

[92]Gunnell, OP. Cit., p.122.

[93]Ben J. Ravsten and Eunice P. Ravsten, *History of Clarkston, The Granary of Cache Valley* (Logan, Utah: Unique, 1966) p.172.

[94]Caroline Harris' application for pension, 1879; in possession of Belle H. Wilson.

[95]Ibid.

[96]Ibid.

[97]Obituary, *Deseret News:* Jan. 27, 1888), p. 2; quoting from *The Logan Journal*.

[98]Harris Family Records, in possession of the authors.

[99]William H. Homer, Jr., ". . . Publish It Upon the Mountain," *Improvement Era*, July, 1955. pp.505–506.

[100]Edward Stevenson, "One of the Three Witnesss," *Millennial Star*, vol. 44, Nov. 30, 1880; p. 86.

[101]*Millenial Star*, vol. 48, 1886, p. 78.

[102]Edward Stevenson, *Millenial Star*, vol. I, p. 86.

[103]Edward Stevenson, *Millenial Start*, vol. I, p.

[104]Journal History, June 1, 1877, pp.1–2.

[105]Journal History, Oct. 10, 1870, p. 1.

[106]Edward Stevenson, in letter form, Stevenson's "Private Journal" XXXII, *Deseret News*, Dec. 13, 1881: quoted from pages 163–164 of "Stevenson's Family History" by Joseph Grant Stevenson, compiler, (Provo, Utah: Stevenson's Publishing Co., 1955). Used by permission of Joseph Grant Stevenson.

[107]Andrew Jensen's Church Chronology, p. 84, under date.

[108]Harris Reunion minutes, Aug. 3, 1928.

[109]Autobiograpy of William Pilkington, p. 11.

[110]William H. Homer, July 1955, p. 506, quotes Geo. Q. Cannon. Editorial in *Deseret News*, Sept. 7, 1870.

[111]Ole A. Jensen, "Notarized Statement", *History of Clarkston, The Granary of Cache County*.

[112]Pilkington.

[113]Contributed by Maurine R. Westover, 1860, Peach Place, Concord, Calif. 94518; copy in possession of Belle H. Wilson.

[114]Pilkington, pp.7–8.

[115]Willaim H. Homer, Jr., *Improvement Era*, 1926, p. 472, and July 1955, pp.52–25.

[116]*Biographical Encyclopedia*, vol. I, p. 276.

[117]Joseph Smith, Sr., to Martin Harris, Patriarchal Blessing, p. 32.

[118]Autostat of copy found in Martin Harris' file in Church Historical Department.

[119]William H. Homer, Jr., talk at family reunion; recorded in family records.

BIBLIOGRAPHY

Martin Harris

Anderson, Richard Lloyd. *Investigating the Book of Mormon Witnesses.* Salt Lake City: Deseret Book Co., 1981.

Andrus, Hyrum L. and Helen Mae. *They Knew The Prophet.* Salt Lake City: Bookcraft, Inc., 1974.

Bean, Willard, A.B.O. *History of Palmyra.* Palmyra, N.Y.: Palmyra Courier Co., Inc. 1938.

Cook, Thomas L. *Palmyra and Vicinity.* Palmyra, New York.

Deseret News. Salt Lake City: Deseret News Press, 1888.

Ensign, July 1980.

Fresh, Robert, president of The Cobblestone Society and Head Curator of the Rochester Museum. Lecture, Jan. 20, 1977.

Gregg, Thomas. *The Prophet of Palmyra*, New York: John B. Alden, 1890.

Gunnell, Wayne Cutler, "Martin Harris, Witness & Benefactor To the Book of Mormon," B.Y.U., June 1955. (Includes the copy of William Pilkington's manuscript.)

Homer, William H., Jr. ". . . Publish It Upon the Mountain." *Improvement Era*, July 1955.

Homer, William H., Jr. "The Passing of Martin Harris," *Improvement Era, vol. 29, 1926.*

James, Rhett S. *"The Man Who Knew: The Life of Martin Harris,"* a musical pageant.

Journal History. Salt Lake City: The Church of Jesus Christ of Latter-day Saints, Historical Department, 1877)

Kimball, Stanley B. "The First Road West." *Ensign*, Jan. 1979.

Knight, Lydia. Homespun. Noble Women's Lives Series. Salt Lake City: Juvenile Instructor Office, 1883, pp. 98-99.

Linschoten, Eldon K., "A Look at the Newly Discovered Joseph Smith Manuscript," *Ensign*, July 1980, pp.69–73; photography inside front and back covers.

Lundwall, N.B., compiler. *Temples of the Most High*. Salt Lake City: Zion's Printing and Publishing Co., 1941.

Lyons, Book H., Early Ontario County, *New York Court Records*, New York, 1825.

Millennial Star. Manchester, England, vols. 25, 27, 44.

Old Newspapers II, vols. 22, 24, 25. Palmyra, New York: Palmyra Courier, 1830.

Palmyra Courier, journal. Palmyra, New York: Courier Press, 1872, 1930.

Phelps, William. *Evening and Morning Star*, Independence, Missouri, 1831. Collection of The Church of Jesus Christ of Latter-day Saints, Historical Department.

Ravsten, Ben J. and Eunice P. *History of Clarkston, The Granary of Cache County*. Logan, Utah: Unique, 1966.

Roberts, Brigham H. *A Comprehensive History of the Church*. Salt Lake City: Bookcraft, Inc., 1968.

The Saints Herald, Plano, Ill. Oct. 1, 1879, "The Last Testimony of Sister Emma."

Smith, Don Carlos. *Times and Seasons*. Nauvoo, Illinois, 181, 1849. Collection of The Church of Jesus Christ of Latter-day Saints, Historical Department.

Smith, Joseph, Jr. *History of the Church*. vols. I, II. Salt Lake City, Utah: Deseret News Press, 1902.

Smith, Lucy Mack. *History of Joseph Smith*. Edited by Preston Nibley. Salt Lake City, Utah: Stevens and Wallis, 1945.

Stevenson, Edward. Private Journal XXXII, Sept. 4, 1870. A letter included in Stevenson's Family History, by Joseph Grant Stevenson, Provo, Utah 1955.

Taylder, T.W.P. *The Mormon's Own Book*, 1855; in Special Collections, Harold B. Lee Library, Brigham Young University. See James, Rhett S.

Tucker, Pomroy. *Origin & Rise and Progress of Mormonism, Palmyra, N.Y.* New York: D. Appleton and Co., 1867.

Turner, Orsamus G. *Phelps and Gorham's Purchase.* Rochester, New York: W. Alling, 1851.

Wayne County, New York, Records. Deed Book H. Collected documents at Lyons, New York, 1829.

Wayne Sentinal. Palmyra, New York: Palmyra Free Press, 1831.

Unpublished Materials

Decker, Isaac. "Document." Salt Lake City, Utah: Collection of The Church of Jesus Christ of Latter-day Saints, Historical Department.

Chapter VI

Biography of Emer Harris,
Early Missionary
and Patriarch

EMER HARRIS

Early Missionary and Patriarch

Emer, being the oldest of eight children of Nathan and Rhoda Lapham Harris, natives of Providence, Rhode Island, witnessed the many moves and pioneering of his family as they lived in several counties of upper New York State, as the new frontier beckoned to them after the War for Independence.

Emer was born May 29, 1781, in Cambridge, Washington County, New York. He was twelve years old when he moved with his parents and seven younger brothers and sisters to Palmyra, Ontario County (now Wayne County), New York, in 1793.

No doubt he worked alongside his father and younger brothers, Martin, Preserved, Solomon, and Seville, as they fenced and cultivated the acreage Nathan had purchased from John Swift.

In his later years, Russel King Homer, an early convert to the Mormon Church, was fond of telling his grandchildren experiences of his childhood. He said that when the farmers were clearing and leveling their land, they sometimes uncovered old burial mounds and unearthed heaps of human bones. The young boys used to use the longest ones for ball bats or to build little barns, corrals, and little rail fences.

Chipman Turner, an early resident of Ontario Co., New York, describes the pioneering efforts of the people who first settled the area. In the book *Pioneers of Macedon*, compiled by Mary Louise Eldridge, he told of the construction of their early homes: "The pioneer first secured a contract for his land and then raised a rude log cabin. He had a chimney built of sticks with straw mixed with mud for mortar. He made the roof of elm bark, the floor of split logs and the door of hewn planks. The small window was made of oiled paper. His household goods were brought on an ox sled over a rough underbrushed road to his new home. Often taking weeks to move from his former state." (pp.7–8).

An interesting anecdote is told of Nathan Harris, Emer's father:

"Mr. Harris was a noted hunter and fisherman. At one time in a single haul of a seine in 1792, across Ganargua Creek, resulted in a catch of eighteen fine salmon." At the time Mr. [Nathan] Harris came here only a trail led to his log cabin . . .

Northwest from the house on the west side of the road, was a spring in which Harris kept a pet trout. One day a friend possessed of a large red nose; called on a visit. A social glass was followed by a stroll over the farm and ultimately they came to the spring. The friend got down on all fours for a drink of water, while Harris looked on. As the red nose neared the water, out sprang the trout and seized it; while on the instant an upward toss of the head landed the fish full ten feet to the rear. Harris returned the trout to the spring and informed his bewildered friend that the time was propitious for fishing, and a fine lot was taken that afternoon. The name "Trout Harris," given in consequence of this incident, became widely known.[1]

At twenty-one years of age, Emer married Roxanna Peas, supposedly of Palmyra, New York. Their marriage took place July 22, 1802.

Nathan sold parts of his 600 acres to his sons as they grew to manhood and needed land for homes and their growing families. Emer purchased 50 acres from his father for 200 dollars on January 2, 1806, and another parcel of land February 17, 1807, calling Emer a yeoman, meaning a landowner. The acreage and price were not stated. County records show that Nathan, and sons Emer and Martin, bought and sold land to each other several times.[2].

Six children were born to Emer and Roxanna Peas Harris. Within a few years, Emer moved his family to Luzerne Couty, Pennsylvania, where in 1818 he and Roxanna obtained a divorce, ending their marriage of sixteen years.[3] The records do not state the reason for this separation or any information about division of property or custody of the children. Some have supposed it was because of Emer's early affiliation with the Mormon Church, but the date of the divorce discredits this supposition.

On January 16, 1819, Emer married Deborah Lott, the daughter of Zephaniah and Rachel Brown Lott of Luzerne County, Pennsylvania.[4] That fall, Emer purchased shares in a saw mill located on Mehoopany Creek, Luzerne County. He agreed to pay 300 dollars in three payments of 100 dollars down and 100 dollars each year for two years. The final payment was to be paid June 1, 1823. It was agreed that all or part of the payments could be made in lumber "at the market price" or in cash.[5] Thus it was that the four children born to Emer and Deborah Lott Harris came into the world at Mehoopany Creek, near Windham, Luzerne County, Pennsylvania.

Emer Harris, Jr., was born in November 1819, "was dressed and died."[6] Martin Henderson Harris was born September 29, 1820, "at Mehoopany Creek which empties into the Susquehanna River."[7] A daughter, Harriet Fox Harris, was born December 26, 1822. Dennison Lott Harris arrived January 17, 1825, and when but a few weeks old was left motherless.

Emer stated these events very briefly in his almanac (journal)[8]:

22 Dec. 1824	Dr. E.C. saw wife
17 Jan. 1825	had a child born
6 Mar. 1825	wife died
8 Mar. 1825	wife buryed
3 Apr. 1825	took the children to Lu Gary's wife.

A year later, on March 29, Emer married for the third time, Parna Chapell, daughter of Isaac and Tamison Wilcox Chappell, who were residents of Luzerne County and possibly neighbors of Emer's. Parna was then thirty-four years of age, a lovely spinster, willing to become the step-mother of Emer's three small children. She was the only mother they ever remembered, and they honored her with that title. The following January 21, 1827, Parna gave birth to her own little daughter, Fannie Melvina.[9]

That summer the family moved seven miles up Mehoopany Creek to a new farm.[10] It was probably while Emer was living in this location that he had contact with his younger brother, Martin, who was acting as scribe for Joseph Smith from April to June 1828 at Harmony, Pennsylvania, in the translation of the Book of Mormon. Family tradition says that Emer walked twenty-five miles to hear more about the new "golden Bible" from his brother. The location of Emer's farm would have been about that distance from Harmony (now Oakland), Pennsylvania.

Martin's vibrant enthusiasm left a lasting impression on Emer. Subsequent contacts have been blotted out by time, but Emer was sufficiently impressed with the reports of the "new religion" that he found himself making his way back to Palmyra to learn more. He was with Martin as the first bound copy of the Book of Mormon came off the Grandin Press on March 26, 1830. Martin picked up the book and presented it to his older brother, Emer.[11] (The first edition was bound in brown pigskin. The book measured 1½ inches by 4½ inches by 8 inches, with no division or numbering or verses, but was divided into chapters, broken into frequent paragraphs. This volume is now in the Deseret Book Company vault.)

As one studies the geography of this area, one finds that travel across Lake Cayuga and canals made Palmyra within a few days travel from Emer's home in Pennsylvania.

The sixth of April 1830 was a memorable date as The Church of Jesus Christ of Latter-day Saints was formally organized with the legally required six members at the home of Peter Whitmer, at Fayette, Seneca County, New York. On July 19, 1830, Parna gave birth to Joseph Mormon Harris, said to be the first child born to converted Latter-day Saint parents.[12] Howevr, Emer's baptism did not take place until February 19, 1831, an event recorded in Newel Knight's Journal: "Bro. Hyrum Smith, wife and family, came to Colesville [New York] to live with me, but most of his time, as also that of my own, was spent in the villages around, preaching the gospel wherever we could find any one who would listen to us, either in public or private. A few believed and were baptized, among whom was Emer

1830 FIRST EDITION OF THE
BOOK OF MORMON

The book pictured here is one of the first copies of the Book of Mormon printed in Palmyra, New York in March 1830.

After completing his translation of the ancient plates containing the record of the Book of Mormon, Joseph Smith contracted with Mr. Egbert B. Grandin of Palmyra to print 5,000 copies of the book for the sum of $3,000.00. The money for the printing was furnished by Martin Harris, who was one of the three special witnesses who testified to the book's truthfulness.

This particular copy of the first edition was given by Martin Harris to his brother, Emer Harris, who later gave it to his daughter, Elvira Harris Mosier, wife of Benjamin Moser (Elvira's mother was Roxanna Peas Harris).

Elvira Mosier gave the book to her son, Edwin P. Mosier, who inscribed his name in the book. Edwin's wife, Ruth Pierce Bryant Mosier, gave the book to her granddaughter, Lillian Franks Magee, wife of Bert Lee Magee. Their son, Reginald Herschall Magee, received the book from his parents. It was from Reginald that Deseret Book (through its agent in Glendale, California, namely William E. Rounds) obtained the copy and received verification of its transfer from generation to generation.

The small black book also shown here is a book of common prayer, owned by Nathan Harris, father of Martin and Emer. It bears his signature in two places, along with the statement: "His Book, Kirtland, Ohio, A.D. 1833."

These books are now in a vault at Deseret Book Co. in Salt Lake City, who gave permission to family members Madeline S. Mills, Belle H. Wilson and Madge H. Tuckett to take the accompanying picture in March 1979.

Harris, brother to Martin Harris, who proved to be a useful laborer in the vineyard.[13]" From this day forward, Emer, Parna, and family cast their lots with the body of the Church and participated in the subsequent trials, travels, and tribulations connected with it.

When the early gathering place for the Church was designated as Kirtland, Ohio, Emer and family complied with the directive in the early spring of 1831.

According to the Harris Journal:

> Started for Kirtland, Geauga Co., Ohio. Traveled about seventy miles by land and took steamboat at Ithaca [New York] head of the Cayuga Lake. Traveled by steamer about 36 miles; thence through Palmyra, Rochester and Lockport by the Erie Canal to Buffalo, then took passage on the schooner "Constitution" up Lake Erie, intending to land at Fairport [Ohio] but on account of an unfavorable wind were obliged to pass by, and land at Cleveland thence 25 miles by land to the Isaac Morley Farm near Kirtland and near the little Chagrin River five or six miles from Lake Erie.[14]

Newel Knight's group of the Colesville branch of about sixty Saints left for Kirtland in early April, 1831. The description of their journey closely parallels those of Emer Harris. It is likely they met by appointment at Ithaca and thereafter traveled together. Martin Harris' group of fifty Saints left Palmyra May 27, 1831, and arrived in Kirtland in June, having been preceded by Mother Smith's group, who arrived there also in May.[15]

Emer and family established a residence in Brownhelm, Lorain County, Ohio, and while attending the Church conference in Orange, Cuyahoga County, October 25, 1831, Emer was ordained a high priest by order of Joseph Smith.[16] At this same conference the following appointment was made October 27, 1831: "Emer Harris, scribe for Joseph Smith, while they are employed writing and copying the fullness of the scriptures; 'We do therefore most cheeerfully recommend to you and the Grace of God, our beloved brother, Emer Harris who has been appointed and ordained to that office by this conference.' "[17]

Emer Harris was in attendance when the Church met for its conference in Amhurst, Ohio, on January 25, 1832, and the Prophet Joseph Smith was sustained and ordained President of the High Priesthood. Along with many others, Emer was called to fulfill a mission for the Church: "Wherefore, let my servant Simeon Carter and my servant Emer Harris be united in the ministry" (D&C 75:30). Emer left for his mission either just before or soon after the birth of his son Alma, who was born June 2, 1832.

An account of missionary labors given by Newel Knight was published in the *Evening and Morning Star.* It reads as follows:"Dec. 21, 1832 . . . brothers Martin and Emer Harris have baptized 100 persons at Chenango Point; N.Y., [south of Oneida Lake] within a few weeks past."[18] They also organized a branch of the Church with 70 persons at Springville, Susquehanna County, Pennsylvania."[19]

Letters from Emer's field of labor disclose many of his activities and his high degree of spirituality. The following is a letter dated May 7, 1833, written from Springville, Pennsylvania.

To: Mr. George James or Mrs. Parna Harris, Brownhelm, Lorain, Ohio. Dearly beloved Brethren: grace, mercy & pease be multlied unto you that are in the Lord. And to all that are sanktified in Like faith. I have had a desire for a long time to write unto you & also to hear from you. But more partickalar to see you that I might be filled with your company & impart unto you by the word of mouth of my travels and Labors since I left you of which I can tell but little with pen & ink. Brother Martin is with me & has been the grater part of the time since we left Kirtland. We have traveled mutch & Preached mutch. Eighty two have been baptised and many more have believed. We find no end to the call for our labours And many miracles have been done in the Name of Jesus Christ & signs follow them that believe . . . [Writing too blurred] . . . I have not been sick but the part of one day since I left you. I have not suffered by cold nor hunger, But have found many kind friends who have administered unto my necesetys. Altho we have found many apposers & bitter Enimyes, the Lord reward them according to their deed. The 24th of Last January Bro. Martin [Harris] was taken a prisenor on a fals charge of standen & went to prison a few days until we got Bail to answer to Cort the Last Monday in April, or we should probably have been to the Ohio before this time. But it is now put over until the next September tirm; therefore we shall take up our journey Westward are long & go as the Lord shall direct until we arive in the Ohio. Whether the work be mutch or little on the way thither, we cannot tell, the will of the Lord be done, therefore, we cannot tell what time we may be expected there. The work of the Lord is prospering where ever we can hear. We are cretabbly informed that a man had wrote a letter from Canada to Ithaca where he lived two years ago that he belonged to a Mormonite Church of 250 members in Canada . . . Dear Brethern of Brownhelm, Pray for me that I may have my mouth open to speak sutch things as I aught to speak & that I may have a safe return to you in the Lords one [own] due time And I will try to pray for you. Truly it is a day of sacenefising & the tithing of his people but they that are tithed shall not be burned. Prias the Lord for his goodness. Continue in the faith unto the end . . . [writing too blurred] . . . Praise Him ye saints & give him all the glory. And we will praise him again when we pass over masoury [Missouri] Dear Brethern, I will send you a few lines composed by a sister of the Church of [Jesus] Christ a day or two after Bro. Martin was sent to jail on the occasion of his imprisenment. [Poem printed in Martin's history.]

To all the Brothers & Sisters in the Lord At Brownhelm, Lorain Co., Ohio, Springville, May 7th 1833 So I remain your unworthy Brother in the Lord [Signed] Emer Harris[20]

The following is a copy of the letter written from Springville, Pennsylvania, to Emer's wife, Parna:

Dear Wife, my best respects to you & the children and may the Lord bless you all. I have longd to hear from you and to know how you got along both timerally & spiritually but more to see you & our little son. Parna, I have not received any letter from you. When I wrote to Kirtland & directed them to write to you to let you know how I did & where I was & also to inform you that I woud write to you often. I have been to Windham. I have been also to the head of Towanda Creek, have seen all your folks But as Tacy said she would write to you I shall not say any more concerning them now. I will now speak of our old neighbours they are generally full of hardness & unbelief. Hatfield is firm in the faith, his wife has been Baptised. Jonthan Farr, Lenard Lott and Eligah Fossett Sen. are dead & Taylor has had a child drowned. Lydia Farr is married to Jessey Clapp they have a child 5 or 6 months old. My farm is sold for 550 Dollers I was to have one half of the pay this spring the remainder next but I shall not be able [to] get any mony at all on the accout of the dry wether so that their is no runing of Lumber to get mony, the dry wether still continues. Parna, I must now conclude my letter by sending you a few lines composed by a sister of the Church for you

1. Now come Dear handmaid of the Lord
   Come listen to the gospel word
   The Lord commands your Husband go
   And says the gospel trumpet blow

2. Now he is cald to leave his home
   Ore braud creation for to rome
   An all the Nations for to call
   And Preach the blessed news to all

3. The Lord stand by you in your fears
   And he will wipe your falling tears
   And teach you all his holy will
   That He's the blessed Savior still

4. And he will guide you with his hand
   And bring you to join Zions land
   And if on earth you no more meet
   Its there your joy will be compleat

5. Then O Dear Sister do not faint
   The Lord will hear your souls complaint
   O pray to him from day to day
   And then your faith will not decay

6. He lives to hear your feable cryes
   He lives to wipe your weeping Eyes
   Then prais him in the highest strains
   He is the King of Kings who reigns.

   Farewell Dear Wife till we shall meet again, give my respects to all inquiring friends, so I remain your affectionate Husband [Signed] Emer Harris[21]

Midsummer 1833, Emer returned from his mission, having been gone "one year lacking eleven days." His son later wrote, "About Christmas moved onto a farm father [Emer] had bought about seven miles distant in Florence Township, Huron County, Ohio, by the side of the Vermillio River."[22] Here they were privileged to plant crops and harvest them for a few years before moving on. On July 2, 1834, a son, Charles, was born to them.[23]

In the fall of 1835 Emer went to work on the Kirtland Temple. He was a skilled carpenter and joiner, having learned the trade early in life. He was responsible for making the window sash in the temple and for other intricate details within the sacred building.

Details are unknown concerning the lives and activities of Emer's parents, Nathan and Rhoda Harris, during those years when their three sons and one daughter were affiliating themselves with the newly established Church of Jesus Christ. In 1833, Nathan and Rhoda were in Mentor, Lake County, Ohio, just a few miles north of Kirtland, staying at the home of their son, Preserved, also an early baptized convert. Martin and Emer had established homes nearby while Naomi and her husband, Ezekiel Kellogg, were probably in Missouri.

On November 18, 1835, Joseph Smith, his wife, his mother, and his scribe drove to Mentor, where the Prophet preached the funeral sermon for "the father of Preserved Harris. The Prophet preached on the subject of the Resurrection."[24]

According to the Harris record, they moved again: "In the spring of 1836, gave up the farm and were moved by Moses [Judson] Dailey onto the Foy Farm about three miles from the town of Kirtland on the Chardon road. Rented the farm of ten acres for one year for 30 dollars. Summer cold and wet. Raised poor crops but had plenty of apples."[25]

Being near Kirtland, Emer and his family and his brothers and their families surely must have attended the dedication of the Kirtland Temple on April 3, 1836. However, in June following the dedication, Preserved was called before the High Council of Kirtland on charges of " 'a want of benevolence to the poor, and charity to the Church;' and the hand of fellowship was withdrawn from him."[26] In September the following year, Martin was dropped from the High Council. To see his two brothers reprimanded by the Church was a great sorrow to Emer, but he sustained those in authority and carried on his own life and works. Martin, having repented, was rebaptized on November 7, 1842, but Preserved never did reaffiliate himself with the Church.

In the spring of 1838, after the crops were in, Emer returned to Pennsylvania to get the pay for his property that he had left there. He returned in July with a span of horses and a light wagon. His son wrote, "[Father] bought

*"After searching the chest, they tapped the bottom
and found it solid and soon were on their way. The
precious books were undiscovered."*

another horse and a two horse wagon from [his] brother, Preserved."[27]

On September 5, 1838, Emer and his family started for Missouri, the new land of Zion for the Latter-day Saints. "Passed through Columbus the capital of Ohio, through Indianapolis the capital of Indiana and through Springfield the capital of Illinois. Crossed the Mississippi at Louisiana [Pike County, Missouri] and arrived at the house of Uncle Ezekiel Kellogg about the 12 of Oct."[28]

The mob ordered all Mormons to leave Missouri within one month and go east or they would put into effect Governor Boggs' Order of Extermination.

About October 27, Emer and his family started for Quincy, Illinois, a hundred miles east. Among their meager possessions was a chest containing copies of the Book of Mormon. Emer had fitted the books under a false bottom, lined with Fuller's cloth, in case they were searched by the mobs, who had threatened to destroy every Book of Mormon they found.

As a mob approached (said to be four hundred on horseback), Emer walked away from the wagon carrying his gun and ammunition, knowing that if the mob found weapons, it would mean punishment and loss of the gun, so much needed for protection and food. Parna, Emer's wife, was stopped by the mob and asked if she were a "Mormon." Her fearless reply was, "Yes, and thank God for it." She was told that they had authority to search her wagon. She told them to go ahead, saying, "You have driven us from place to place until we have nothing left but rags." The captain, who was on a beautiful horse, made the remark, "Well, you certainly are a brave woman, at least." He then took her little son, Alma, age six, and seated him upon his horse while he searched their possessions saying, "It is a shame to put him down in the snow in his bare feet." After searching the chest; they tapped the bottom and found it solid and soon were on their way. The precious books were undiscovered.[29]

The chest with a false bottom in which
"Books of Mormon" were hidden

False bottom chest with grandsons of Emer Harris.

They traveled on, as Emer's son Martin H. Harris recorded: "Arriving on the banks of the Mississippi about the 12th of November having traveled the whole distance through rain, mud and snow. Remained there until about the 22nd before we could cross on account of floating ice. At this time we crossed the river and went up to Whipple's Mill about one mile distant and staid there until about the first of December; when we moved into the home of John Gault near Rock Creek about eight miles north of Quincy, in Adams County [Illinois]."[30]

Emer became ill from exhaustion and exposure due to the terrible experiences of the expulsion from Missouri. He and his family remained near Quincy for about a year while he recovered from his illness. His sons took care of the planting and harvesting on the rented farm, noting that they bought two cows costing twenty dollars each.

The summer of 1840, Emer "went up to Nauvoo about 40 miles distant and bought a claim of 40 acres in the timber; about three miles northeast from Nauvoo. . . . This fall went up and cut some hay and commenced improvements and built a house. Early in the spring of 1841 we moved onto our new place. Made rails and fenced in about half of it. Broke up and planted and sowed some 8 or 10 acres."[31]

About this time Emer's sons Martin H. and Dennison joined the Nauvoo Legion along with hundreds of other able-bodied men and were present at the laying of the cornerstone of the Nauvoo Temple April 6, 1841. That summer Emer worked on the temple, continuing to do so until the expulsion of the Saints. He is credited with building the winding stairway.

Sorrow came to the family December 7, 1841, with the death of their fourteen-year-old daughter, Fannie Melvina. Life had been difficult for young children growing up in the many years of persecution and privation. This is forcibly brought to mind when one views the 1842 Hancock County Tax assessment of Emer Harris (tenant), Section 20, Appanoose Township.[32]

Cattle — $50
Horses — none

Wagons — $50
Clocks — none
Watches — none
Money loaned — none
Stock in trade — none
Other personal property — 30

Total Value — $130.00

Emer resided in Appanoose Township, where the Church census of 1842 listed him, his wife Parna, and his son Charles (age eight years) in one household. The older sons were probably living and working elsewhere.

It was during the Nauvoo years that Emer's son Dennison was involved in reporting the mob's plots to murder the Prophet.[33] (This story is told in detail in the history of Dennison Lott Harris, to follow.)

On June 11, 1843, Parna entered the water to be baptized by proxy for her daughter Fannie. This ordinance was performed in the Nauvoo font in the otherwise unfinished temple.[34]

The Harris family along with all other loyal Latter-day Saints was called upon to endure the tragedy of the martyrdom of their beloved leader and prophet on June 27, 1844. Young Charles preserved the memory of the mantle of the Prophet falling on Brigham Young by saying in youthful phrasing, "It nearly scared the hell out of me." Perhaps it did, because for all his long life he endeavored to live the principles of the gospel.[35]

Early in 1845, Emer took as a plural wife thirty-three year old Polly Chamberlain, daughter of a neighbor, Solomon Chamberlain, a stalwart in the Church since the days of Palmyra. To this union was born on December 24, 1845, a little daughter, Rebecca.[36]

Emer served as president of the Woodland Branch of the Church, Ward II, with thirty-six members. Once a week a general meeting was held in Nauvoo. All other meetings were held in the branch.

Parna Harris received her patriarchal blessing from John Smith October 21, 1845. This proved to be a great comfort to her as it pronounced a promise: ". . . that thou mayest be restored to sound health as in the days of thy youth, that thou mayest be made useful in thy family and in the church and kingdom of Jesus Christ."[37]

At last the long-awaited day arrived when the Saints in Nauvoo were privileged to go to the temple to receive their endowments. For Emer and Parna, it was January 30, 1846.[38] This event proved to be a sustaining influence in the trials of the exodus so soon to follow.

The Harris family left their home along with other Saints expelled from Nauvoo in the fall of 1846. Eventually, Emer and his wife Parna, several sons, Polly, and the baby, Rebecca, arrived in Pottawattamie County, Iowa. Once more Emer established a humble home and tried to make the best of difficult circumstances. He witnessed the calling of the Mormon Battalion at Winter Quarters in July, 1846, and the departure of the original pioneers on April 16, 1847, headed for the Rocky Mountains.

The Saints anxiously awaited the return that fall of members of the pioneer vanguard to report the founding of a permanent settlement in the tops of the western domain. Brigham Young and about a hundred men returned on October 22, 1847, to Winter Quarters, where Brigham remained until the following summer.

In early December, 1847, a conference of the Church was called, but because the building was not large enough to accommodate the crowd, Brigham proposed that a "Log Tabernacle" be erected. So on December 24 they reconvened at Council Bluffs in a hastily built 60-foot by 45-foot edifice that accommodated a thousand persons. It was here that the business took place of reorganizing the First Presidency with Brigham Young as president of the Church, with counselors — Heber C. Kimball and Willard Richards and twelve apostles.[39]

The conference lasted several days, and soon afterwards, Emer requested that Brigham Young perform the sealing ordinance for his previous marriage to Polly Chamberlain. This was done at Winter Quarters on January 11, 1848, witnessed by Heber C. Kimball and Newel K. Whitney, the Presiding Bishop of the Church.[40]

131

About six months later, Emer received a patriarchal blessing from John Smith. An excerpt follows:

> Thou has not fainted in times of disease and persecution when every evil thing has [been] spoken against the church of the Living God. Thou hast endured in faith. The Lord is well pleased with thee because of the integrity of thy heart. He will heap a multiplicity of blessings on thy head. . . . Thy testimony shall have great weight among all people because of thy candor. The simplicity of thy manner of communicating it, and because thou art alone, as it were, in thy father's house. . . . Thou shalt be able to control the hearts of thy friends and save them and reign over them, notwithstanding they think their counsel greater than thou.[41]

At the time this blessing was given, Emer was living at Kanesville, not far from Winter Quarters, Iowa. When the conference for the Church was held October 21, 1848, all assembled were surprised to see Oliver Cowdery and his family in attendance. Oliver had been absent from the Church, old friends, and associates for eleven years. During this time, he had been plagued by ill health and financial reverses.

He asked to be taken once again into membership in the Church he had helped, from the writing of the manuscript for the Book of Mormon, as translated by the Prophet Joseph Smith, to the restoration of the priesthood and the organization of the Church. Upon being invited to address the congregation, he bore an inspiring testimony. He requested rebaptism and expressed a desire to join the saints in the Great Salt Lake Valley.. Emer Harris, along with the other Saints, sustained the action to accept him back into the fold. Soon afterward, Oliver was rebaptized.

Though Oliver did not live to join the Saints in the West, he "died the happiest man I ever saw,"[42] according to his brother-in-law, David Whitmer.

Sorrow came again to Emer in the passing of Polly, sometime in the early months of 1849. So their young child, Rebecca, was probably placed in the care of her aunt, Naomi H. Kellogg.

On June 14, 1850, Emer's son, Martin H., left for the Great Salt Lake Valley with his step-mother, Parna, and young Alma. Other family members left earlier with the Kelloggs.[43] Emer and his sons Dennison and Charles remained in Iowa. Perhaps they were asked by Church leaders to remain to assist later immigrants.

Emer made and repaired wagons while Dennison did the blacksmithing until the summer of 1852, when most of the Saints, including Dennison and his wife, Sarah, and his three little daughters, finally left Kanesville. The Harrises arrived in Utah in October, 1852, in Captain Cutler's company and immediately became involved in pioneering the State of Deseret. Parna and the older sons were established in Willard near Brigham City, Utah, but Harris homes were eventually established throughout the state.[44]

Emer, then of Provo, Utah, was ordained a patriarch at the General Conference of the Church in Salt Lake City on October 8, 1853, and gave his first blessing in January 1854. This calling he fulfilled until the end of his life.

By midsummer of 1855, all of Emer's older children were married. That fall, on September 10, 1855, he was sealed to Martha Allen by George A. Smith. Martha was the daughter of Josiah and Olive (Negus) Allen. Martha was married in about 1823 to Hawley Decker Smith Markham, by whom she had two children. She was married again in about 1832 to David Henry Orser. They became the parents of six children. Martha became the "step-mother" Rebecca wrote of in her own life story.

On September 2, 1855, Emer was appointed to preside over fifty high priests in Provo, Utah.[45] Distance and difficulty of travel prevented Emer's attendance at the funeral of his wife Parna, who died at the home of her son, Joseph, on June 4, 1857, at Ogden, Utah. After Martha's death in May 1860, young Rebecca went to work in the William Joseph Taylor home in Provo, Utah, and became the plural wife of this good man on November 24, 1860, in the Endowment House. From then until the end of his life, Emer spent time living with his married sons, Martin H., at Harrisville (near Ogden), Joseph and Alma of Ogden and Logan, Dennison and Charles at Willard, and later southern Utah, where they went to help establish settlements in "Utah's Dixie."

Early in 1867, Emer returned to northern Utah. On August 27, 1869, he traveled twenty miles to Salt Lake with his son Martin H. and his daughter Harriet H. Daley, who was to act as proxy for the women relatives as they performed sacred ordinances for their departed dead.

The following day Emer was sealed to Deborah Lott. Harriet H. Daley acted as proxy for her deceased mother. This sealing was performed by Daniel H. Wells and witnessed by Joseph F. Smith and Jonathan Lyon.[46]

For the next few years, Emer lived intermittently with his sons Joseph, Alma, and Martin H. He died while living with Alma in Logan, Utah, on November 28, 1869. Emer was eighty-eight years of age, not having seen his dear brother Martin for thirty-two years. Martin, now reconciled with the Church, arrived in Salt Lake City from Kirtland, Ohio, August 30, 1870, missing an earthly reunion with Emer by nine months.

Emer's earthly resting place is at the Logan City Cemetery, where an appropriate monument declares his virtues in the following manner:

> Emer Harris, born at Cambridge, New York, May 27, 1781. A direct descendant of Thomas Harris who came to America with Roger Williams in 1631 for religious freedom. Through the influence of his brother, Martin, the witness to the Book of Mormon, Emer received the first bound copy. He was baptized into the Church in 1831 by Hyrum Smith. Called on a mission by revelation in 1832 [D&C 75:32] worked on Kirtland and Nauvoo Temples. Came to Utah in 1852. Pioneered Ogden, Provo, and Southern Utah. Was ordained Patriarch in 1853. The father of 15 children. Died in Logan, Utah Nov. 28, 1869 in his 89th year. (Inscription composed by Silas Albert Harris, grandson of Emer Harris, and father of the co-authors, Belle and Madge Harris.)

*Emer Harris Monument
Logan City Cemetery.*

FOOTNOTES

Emer Harris

[1]Thomas L. Cook, *Palmyra and Vicinity*, p. 204.

[2]"Early Ontario Court Records," Lyons, New York, *Deed Books* B., p. 296 and D., p. 282, 1806, 1807.

[3]Franklin S. Harris, Sr., MSS 340, in Special Collections, Harold B. Lee Library, Brigham Young University, Provo, Utah; hereafter cited as "Writings of Emer Harris".)

[4]"Family Record of Emer Harris," March 19, 1868, (in a family publication, *Martin Henderson Harris – A Utah Pioneer*, July 21, 1952), p. 1; hereafter cited as M.H.H.

[5]*Deeds of Luzerne County*, vol. 27, Wilkes Barre, Pennsylvania, 1819, p. 346.

[6]M.H.H., p. 1.

[7]Ibid.

[8]Writings of Emer Harris.

[9]M.H.H., p. 1.

[10]Ibid, p. 12.

[11]Frank Essholm, Pioneers and Prominent Men of Utah, (Salt Lake City, Utah: Utah Pioneer Publishing Co., 1913), p. 919.

[12]Andrew Jensen, *Supplement To Church Chronology*, 1906–1913, May 2, 1909, (Salt Lake City: Deseret News Press, 1914), p. 28.

[13]Incidents from "Newel Knight's Journal" printed in *Scraps of Biography* (Salt Lake City: Juvenile Instructor Office, 1883); pp.65–66.

[14]M.H.H., p.12.

[15]Stanley B. Kimball, "The First Road West," *Ensign*, January 1979, pp. 29–30.

[16]Joseph Smith, Jr., *History of the Church*, vol. I, (Salt Lake City, Utah: L.D.S. Church), p. 219.

[17]*Introduction to Church History*, Historical Department, The Church of Jesus Christ of Latter-day Saints (hereafter cited as Historical Department.)

[18]"William W. Phelps," *Evening and Morning Star*, vol. I, #9, Independence, Missouri, Feb. 1833.

[19]Writings of Emer Harris.

[20]Franklin S. Harris, Sr., in Special Collections, Harold B. Lee Library, Brigham Young University, Provo, Utah.

[21]Ibid.

[22]M.H.H., p.12.

[23]Ibid., p.1.

[24]Smith, Jr., *History of the Church*, vol. II, p. 317.

[25]M.H.H., p.12.

[26]Smith, Jr., *History of the Church*, vol. II, p. 445.

[27]M.H.H., p.13.

[28]Ibid., p.13.

[29]Private letters, papers, and traditions of the Harris family in possession of Belle H. Wilson.

[30]M.H.H., p. 13.

[31]Ibid.

[32]*Introduction to Church History*.

[33]The Contributor, vol. V.

[34]Nauvoo Baptisms for the Dead, alphabetical file, Genealogical Department of the L.D.S. Church (hereafter cited as Genealogical Department).

[35]Harris family oral tradition.

[36]M.H.H., p.1.

[37]John Smith to Parna Harris, Patriarchal Blessing, Oct. 21, 1845, Historical Department, vol. 9, p.435.

[38]Nauvoo Temple Endowment Records, Jan. 30, 1846, Genealogical Department.

[39]Preston Nibley, *Brigham Young* (Salt Lake City: Deseret News Press, 1937), pp.112–13.

[40]Early Sealing Records, special collection of Genealogical Department, F 183374, p.727.

[41]John Smith to Emer Harris, Patriarchal Blessing, July 19, 1848, Historical Department, vol. 9, p.303.

[42]Stanley R. Gunn, *Oliver Cowdery, Second Elder and Scribe* (Salt Lake City: Bookcraft Inc., 1962), p.209.

[43]M.H.H., p.17.

[44]Private letters, papers, and traditions of the Harris family in possession of Belle H. Wilson.

[45]*Journal History*, September 2, 1855, Historical Department.

[46]Endowment House Sealing Records, special collection of Genealogical Department, Aug. 28, 1869.

BIBLIOGRAPHY

Emer Harris

The Contributor, published materials, vol. V, 1884.

Deeds of Luzerne County. Vol. 27, 1819, Wilkes Barre, Pennsylvania.

Early Ontario County, New York Court Records. Deed Books B and D, Lyons, New York; 1806, 1807.

Eldridge, Mary Louise, *Pioneers of Macedan*. Macedan Center, Wayne Co., N.Y., 1912.

Ensign, Jan. 1979.

Essholm, Frank. *Pioneers and Prominent Men of Utah*. Salt Lake City: Utah Pioneer Publishing Co., 1913.

Family Record of Emer Harris, in family publication, *Martin Henderson Harris – A Utah Pioneer*, 1952.

Gunn, Stanley R. *Oliver Cowdery, Second Elder and Scribe*. Salt Lake City: Bookcraft Inc., 1962.

Harris, Franklin S., Sr. In Special Collection, Harold B. Lee Library, Brigham Young University, Provo, Utah.

Jensen, Andres. *Church Chronology*. Salt Lake City: Deseret News Press, 1914.

"Newel Knight's Journal". *Scraps of Biography*. Salt Lake City: Juvenile Instructor Office, 1883.

Nibley, Preston. *Brigham Young*. Salt Lake City: Deseret News Press, 1937.

Phelps, William. *Evening and Morning Star*, 1833, Independence, Missouri.

Smith, Joseph, Jr. *History of the Church*. Salt Lake City, Utah: see Church of Jesus Christ of Latter-day Saints, 1902.

UNPUBLISHED MATERIALS

Early Sealing Records, 1848. Salt Lake City: Collection of The Church of Jesus Christ of Latter-day Saints, Genealogical Department.

Endowment House Sealing Records, 1869. Salt Lake City: Collection of The Church of Jesus Christ of Latter-day Saints, Genealogical Department.

Nauvoo Baptisms for Dead. Salt Lake City: Collection of The Church of Jesus Christ of Latter-day Saints, Genealogical Department.

Nauvoo Temple Endowment Records, 1846. Salt Lake City: Collection of The Church of Jesus Christ of Latter-day Saints, Genealogical Department.

Private letters, papers, and traditions of the Harris family in possession of Belle H. Wilson.

Smith, John, to Emer Harris, Patriarchal Blessing, vol. 9, 1848. Salt Lake City: Collection of The Church of Jesus Christ of Latter-day Saints, Historical Department.

Smith, John, to Parna Harris, Patriarchal Blessing, vol. 9, 1849. Salt Lake City: Collection of The Church of Jesus Christ of Latter-day Saints, Historical Department.

Chapter VII

Biography of Dennison Lott Harris,
Youthful Defender of
the Prophet

DENNISON LOTT HARRIS

Youthful Defender of the Prophet

Dennison Lott Harris, son of Emer and Deborah Lott Harris, was born January 17, 1825, at Windham, Luzerne County, Pennsylvania. On March 6, 1825,[1] when he was three months old, his mother died. According to Emer's journal, "the three children were put in the care of Lu Gary's wife,"[2] but when Emer married Parna Chapell a year later, the children were reunited with their father and thereafter were in the care of their loving stepmother.

Little is known of Dennison's early life beyond the routine activities of a growing boy in the early 1800's. One entry in his father's journal tells that "Dennison's fell in [mill] race 21 June 1826."[3] Emer's history gives other details of the family's experiences in Kirtland, Ohio, and Missouri. It was in Nauvoo, Illinois, however, that Dennison emerged as a loyal and devoted follower of the Prophet Joseph Smith.

The Prophet asked Emer if his son Den (as he was called) could haul water in barrels from the Mississippi River so that the apostles and other Saints could receive their washings ane annointings "as the enemy wouldn't notice what a young boy was doing." Den willingly performed this service.[4]

One day as the Prophet was walking with Emer and young Den, he plced his arm across Emer's shoulder and said, "Brother Harris, this boy will be a leader in your family." Other promises were made too sacred to be recorded, so they are lost to posterity.[5]

Den and his young friend Robert Scott were credited with saving the life of the Prophet during the Nauvoo period. This story was reported in *The Contributor* in 1884, herewith quoted in detail:

> Early in the spring of 1844, a very strong and bitter feeling was aroused against Joseph, among many of his brethren in and around Nauvoo; and some who held high positions in the Church and were supposed to be his best friends, turned against him and

sought by various means in their power to do him injury. Many murmured and complained, and some of the more wicked; even watched their opportunity to take his life. . . .

At length this wicked feeling became so strong and general, among a certain class, that it was resolved to form an organization, or secret combination that would better enable them to accomplish their wicked purposes.

Accordingly a secret meeting was appointed to take place in the new brick home of William Law, Joseph's first counselor, on a certain Sabbath, and invitations to attend it were carefully extended to members of the Church . . . who were disaffected, or in sympathy with these wicked views and desires. Among those who received invitations to attend this meeting was Brother Dennison L. Harris (now the Bishop of Monroe, Sevier County, Utah), then but a young man of seventeen years of age. Austin A. Cowles, at that time a member of the High Council, was one of the leaders in this wicked movement, and being a near neighbor and on intimate terms with Brother Harris, he had given young Dennison an invitation to the secret meeting, and told him also to invite his father, but to be sure and not breathe a word about it to anyone else, and it was to be kept a profound secret. Dennison was much perplexed over the invitation . . ., and certain things that Brother Cowles had told him; and while sitting on his father's woodpile, thinking them over and wondering what he had better do, another young man, named Robert Scott, who lived but a short distance away, came over, sat down on the log, . . . they had been intimate companions for several years; and they had not conversed long before each discovered that the other had something on his mind which troubled him, but which he did not like to reveal. Finally, one proposed that, as they had always been confidants, they now exchange secrets, on condition that neither should reveal what the other had told him.

Both readily agreed to this, and when each had told the other the cause of his anxiety, it proved to be the same — both had received an invitation to the same meeting. Robert Scott, having been raised by William Law, seemed to be almost a member of his family, and on this account had been invited by him to attend the meeting.

"Well, Den," said Robert, after a short pause, "are you going to attend the meeting?"

"I don't know," replied Dennison, "are you?"

"I don't know whether to go or not," said Robert. "Suppose we go in the house and tell your father of his invitation and see what he says about it."

They entered the house and consulted for some time with Dennison's father, Emer Harris, who was a brother to Martin Harris, one of the three witnesses to the Book of Mormon. They informed him of his invitation to the same meeting, and told him many other things that Brother Cowles had told Dennison . . . He, (Emer) immediately went to Joseph's home, a distance of about two and a half miles, and informed him of the whole affair. Joseph listened with interest until he finished, when he said, "Brother Harris, I would advise you not to attend the meetings, nor pay any attention to them. You may tell the boys, however, that I would like to have them go, but I want them to be sure to come and see me before the meeting takes place. I wish to give them some counsel."

Subsequent events showed the wisdom of Joseph in advising Brother Emer Harris not to attend the meeting and selecting young men to do the work he wished to have accomplished. Brother Harris returned and told the boys what Joseph wanted them to do, and they readily agreed to comply with the request. Accordingly, on the next Sunday before the secret meeting took place, Robert and Dennison called at the house of Joseph to learn what he wished them to do. He told them that he desired that they should attend the meeting, pay strict attention, and report to him all the proceedings. . . . He moreover cautioned them to have as little to say as possible, and to avoid giving any offense.

They attended the meeting as desired. There were quite a number present, and the time was mostly occupied in planning how to get at things the best, and effect an organization. Strong speeches were also made against the Prophet, and many lies told to prejudice the minds of those present against him. This portion of the proceedings was not a difficult task, for the element of which the audience was composed was only too susceptible to such evil impressions, and those who spoke were eminently successful in producing . . . [strong] feelings of enmity toward the Prophet, that they might wish to use in accomplishing his overthrow. It seems that the immediate cause of these wicked proceedings was the fact that Joseph had recently presented the revelation on Celestial Marriage to the High Council for their approval, and certain members were bitterly opposed to it, and denounced Joseph as a fallen Prophet, and were determined to destroy him.

The meeting adjourned to convene again on the following Sabbath, and the two young men were invited to attend the next one also, but were cautioned not to tell a soul of what had transpired at the first one. At the first opportunity they called upon Joseph, related to him all that had taken place, and gave him the names of those who had taken part in the proceedings. The leading members among the conspirators were William and Wilson Law, Austin A. Cowles, Francis and Chauncey Higbee, Robert Foster and his brother, two Hicks brothers, and two merchants, Finche and Rollinson, who were enemies to the Church. After hearing their report and asking several questions, which they answered to the best of their knowledge, Joseph said: "Boys, I would like you to accept their invitation and attend the second meeting. But come to me again next Sunday, before the meeting convenes, as I may have something more to say to you before you go."

At the expiration of a week they again went to see Joseph, who gave them the necessary advice, after which they went to the meeting. This time the conspirators were still more vehement in their abusive remarks about Joseph. New crimes that he had committed had been discovered, and the old ones were much magnified. Their accusations were not only against him, but also against his brother, Hyrum and other prominent men in Nauvoo. There seemed to be no end to the wickedness of which these good men were accused, as most of the time until a late hour was occupied by different ones in denouncing and accusing Joseph and his friends of the most heinous crimes. Before the meeting adjourned, however, it was agreed that they should all endeavor to work the matter up as much as possible during the week, that something definite might be accomplished towards effecting a more complete organization without further delay. The next meeting was to convene again on the following Sunday. As the boys had kept quiet and said nothing against any of their proceedings, it was supposed, of course, that they were in sympathy with the movement, and an invitation was accordingly extended for them to attend the next meeting.

As on the previous occasions, the young men watched for a fitting opportunity of reporting to Joseph without arousing the suspicions of any that attended the meeting. He listened attentively to the recital of all that had taken place at the second meeting, after which he said: "Boys, come to me again next Sunday. I want you to attend the next meeting also." The boys promised to do so, and left the room. They kept the meetings and their connection with them, however, a profound secret from the rest of their friends, and at the appointed time again went to the house of Joseph to receive their usual instructions. This time he said to them with a very serious contenance: "This will be your last meeting; this will be the last time that they will admit you to their councils. They will come to some determination, but be sure," he continued, "that you make no covenants, nor enter into any obligations whatever with them. Be strictly reserved, and make no promise either to conspire against me or any portion of the community. Be silent, and do not take any part in their deliberations." After a pause of some moments he added, "Boys, this will be their last meeting, and they may shed your blood, but I hardly think they will, as you are so young. If they do, I will be a lion in their path! Don't flinch. If you have to die, die like men, you will be martyrs to the cause, and your crowns can be no greater. But," he said again, "I hardly think they will shed your blood."

This interview was a long one. Joseph's sensitive feelings were touched by the faith, generosity and love manifested by these young men in their willingness to undertake such a hazardous an enterprise at his bidding. He blessed them and made them precious promises for their sacrifice, and told them if their lives were taken their reward would be all the greater. After leaving Joseph's house with his sincere wishes for their safety, the boys waited anxiously for the time of the meeting to arrive. They fully realized the dangers into which they were about to plunge themselves, yet they did not shrink. They knew it was their duty and they determined to attempt it at all hazards. They were now familiar with the names of the persons conspiring against Joseph, the object they had in view, and many of their plans for accomplishing that object. Moreover, they were supposed by the would-be-murderers to be in perfect sympathy with all their hellish designs; and if, by any circumstances, they should arouse the suspicion that they were present at Joseph's request, or even with his knowledge, their lives in such a crowd would, indeed, be of little value. They determined to trust in the Lord and die rather than betray the Priesthood. Their feelings may be imagined as the time of the meeting drew near, and they started off in the direction of William Law's house, where it was to be held. They certainly displayed faith that every young man in Israel should cultivate.

On arriving at the rendezvous they found to their surprise and discomforture, that the entrance to the house was guarded by men armed with muskets and bayonets. After being scrutinized from head to foot, and carefully questioned, they succeeded in passing the guards and gaining admittance. From this it will be seen that great care was taken to prevent any person from entering, except those whom they knew to be of their party, and ready to adopt any measures that might be suggested against the Prophet Joseph. On entering they found considerable confusion and much counseling among the members of the conspiracy. All seemed determined that Joseph should die, yet objections were raised by some to each of the plans proposed. The Prophet was accused of the most wicked acts, and all manner of evil was spoken of him. Some declared that he had sought to get their wives from them, and had many times committed adultery. They said he was a fallen Prophet, and was leading the people to destruction. Joseph was not the only one against whom they lied. His brother Hyrum and many of the leading men of Nauvoo were accused of being in league with him and sharing his crimes. In the councilings and plannings, considerable time was spent before the meeting was called to order, and anything definite commenced. The boys, however, followed Joseph's instructions, and remained quiet and reserved. This seemed to arouse the suspicions of some that they were not earnestly in favor of their wicked proposals, and some of the conspirators began to take especial pains to explain to the young men the great crimes that Joseph had committed, and the results that would follow if his wicked career were not checked, with a view of convincing them that their severe measures against Joseph were for the best good of the Church, and persuading them to take an active part with them in accomplishing this great good. The two boys, however, sat together quietly, and would simply answer their arguments by saying that they were only young boys, and did not understand such things, and would rather not take part in their proceedings.

As before stated, Brother Scott had been raised in the family of William Law, and the latter pretended great friendship for him on that account, and was very anxious to explain to him the object of the proposed organization, and induce him to join. He would come around and sit beside Robert, put his arm around his neck, and persuade, argue, and implore him to join in their effort to rid the Church of such a dangerous imposter.

At the same time Brother Cowles would sit beside Brother Harris in the same attitude, and labor with him with equal earnestness. The boys, however, were not easily convinced. Still, in their replies and remarks, they carefully tried to avoid giving the least offense or arousing any suspicions regarding the true cause of their presence. They said they were too young to understand the "spiritual wife doctrine," of which Joseph was accused, and many of the other things that they condemned in the Prophet. Joseph had never done them any harm, and they did not like to join in a conspiracy against his life.

"But," they would urge, "Joseph is a fallen Prophet; he receives revelations from the devil, and is deceiving the people, and if something decisive is not done at once to get rid of him, the whole Church will be led by him to destruction." These and many other arguments were vainly brought forth to induce the boys to join them, but they still pretended not to understand nor take much interest in such things. At length they ceased their persuasions, and, things having developed sufficiently, they concluded to proceed with the intended organization.

An oath had been prepared which each member of the organization was now required to take. Francis Higbee, a justice of the peace, sat at a table in one end of the room and administered to each individual separately, in the following manner: The candidate would step forward to the table, take up a Bible which had been provided for the purpose, and raise it in his right hand, whereupon the justice would ask him in a solemn tone, "Are you ready?" And, receiving answer in the affirmative would continue in a tone and manner that struck awe to the minds of the boys as they listened: "You solemnly swear, before God and all holy angels, and these your brethren, by whom you are surrounded, that you will give your life, your liberty, your influence, your all, for the destruction of Joseph Smith and his party, so help you God!" The person being sworn would then say, "I do," after which he would lay down the Bible and sign his name to a written copy of the oath in a book that was lying on the table, and it would be legally acknowledged by the justice of the peace.

The boys sat gazing upon this scene, wondering how intelligent beings who had once enjoyed the light of truth, could have fallen into such depths of wickedness as to be anxious to take such an oath against the Prophet of God and his faithful followers. They also felt no little uneasiness concerning their own fate, and dreaded the moment when the last one should have taken the oath. At length that portion of the business was accomplished, and about 200 persons had taken the oath. Among that number were three women, who were ushered in, closely veiled to prevent being recognized, and required to take the oath. Besides doing this, they also testified that Joseph and Hyrum Smith had endeavored to seduce them, and wished them to become their wives. After making affidavit to a series of lies of this kind, they made their exit through a back door. One of the women, whom the boys suspected as being William Law's wife, was crying, and seemed to dislike taking the oath, but did so as one who feared that the greatest bodily injury would surely follow a refusal.

After the oath had been administered to all but the two boys, Law, Cowles and others again commenced their labors to get them to take it, . . . Arguments, persuasions, and threats were in turn used . . . but in vain. They exhausted their ingenuity in inventing arguments, lies, and inducements to get the boys to unite with their band. "Have you not heard," said they, "the strong testimony of all present against Joseph Smith? Can a man be a true Prophet who would commit adultery? He is a fallen Prophet; and is teaching the people doctrines that his own imagination or lustful desires have invented, or else he received that revelation from the devil. He will surely lead the whole Church to destruction if his career is not stopped. We can do nothing with him by the law, and for the sake of the Church we deem it our solemn duty to accomplish his destruction and rescue the people from this peril. We are simply combining and conspiring to save the Church, and we wish you to join us in our efforts, and share the honors that will be ours. Come, take the oath and all will be well."

"Oh, we are too young," they replied, "to understand or meddle with such things. . . . We came to your meetings because we thought you were our friends and gave us a kind invitation. We did not think there was any harm in it; but if you will allow us to go now we will not trouble any more of your meetings. Joseph Smith has never done us any harm; and we do not feel like injuring him."

"Come, boys," said another of the crowd, "do as we have done. You are young, and will not have anything to do in the affair, but we want you should keep it a secret, and act with us; that's all."

151

"You've got to take that oath, or you'll never leave here alive."

"No," replied the boys in a firm but cool tone, as they rose to leave, "we cannot take an oath like that against any man who has never done us the least injury." They would glady have passed out and escaped the trouble they saw brewing for them; but, as they feared, they were not allowed to depart so easily. One of the band exclaimed in a very determined voice: "No, not by a d--n sight! You know all our plans and arrangements, and we don't propose that you leave in that style. You've got to take that oath, or you'll never leave here alive."

The attention of all was now directed to the two boys, and considerable confusion prevailed. A voice in the crowd shouted, "Dead men tell no tales!" whereupon a general clamor arose for the boys to take the oath or be killed. Even their pretended friends, Cowles and Law, turned against them. "If you do not take that oath," said one of the leading members, in a blood curdling tone, "we will cut your throats." The looks and conduct of the rest showed plainly that he had spoken only what they were ready to execute. It was evident the mob were eager for blood. That moment certainly must have been a trying one, but it seemed that fear had suddenly vanished from the bosom of the two boys, and they coolly but positively again declared that they would not take an oath nor enter into any other movement against the Prophet Joseph Smith. The mob was now enraged, as they thought they were betrayed, and it was with the greatest difficulty that the leaders succeeded in keeping them from falling upon the boys and cutting them to pieces. The leaders, however, were no less determined that the boys should die, but as the house in which the meeting was held stood but a short distance back from the street, they thought it better to be more quiet about it, lest someone might be passing and discover what was going on. Order was at last restored when it was decided to take the boys down into the cellar where the deed could be more safely accomplished. Accordingly, a guard, with drawn swords and bowie knives, was placed on either side of the boys, while two others, armed with cocked muskets and bayonets, . . . brought up the rear as they marched off in the direction of the cellar. William and Wilson Law, Austin Cowles, and others, accompanied them to the cellar. Before commiting the murderous deed, however, they gave the boys one more chance for their lives. One of them said: "Boys, if you will take that oath your lives shall be spared; but you know too much for us to allow you to go free, and if you are still determined to refuse, we will have to shed your blood." But the boys, with commendable courage, in the very jaws of death, once more rejected the only means that would save their lives. At this juncture, when it seemed that each moment would end the earthly existence of the two noble young men, a voice from some one in the crowd, as if by Divine interposition, called out just in time to save their lives. "Hold on! Hold on there! Let's talk this matter over before their blood is shed!" and with great difficulty some of the more cautious ones succeeded in quieting those whose anger and excitement prevented them from weighing well what they were on the verge of committing, and considering the consequences that would inevitably follow. Thus the instantaneous death of the boys was prevented, while the crowd retreated to the further end of the room and consulted earnestly together, in so low a tone, however, that the boys could not hear what was said. It was evident, however, that they were nearly equally divided in their views of the feasibility of putting the boys to death. Some appeared to be enraged and fully determined to shed their blood, while others were [opposed], . . . [but] . . . the boys distinctly heard one of them say: "The boys' parents very likely know where they are, and if they do not return home, strong suspicions will be aroused, and they may institute a search that would be very dangerous to us. It is already late, and time that the boys were home."

This was a very important consideration, as well as a very unexpected circumstance in favor of the boys. Hope rose high in their breasts as the discussion continued, and one by one of the more excited conspirators was silenced, if not convinced, until at length the tide turned in favor of the boys and it was decided that they should be released. Some openly, and many in their feelings, opposed this resolution, as they considered it as unsafe to liberate the boys to reveal all their plans, as to kill them and get them out of the way.

A strong guard was provided to escort them to a proper distance, lest some of the gang might kill them before they made their escape. They placed a strict injunction upon the boys not to reveal anything they had seen or heard in these meetings, and declared if they did any member of the conspiracy would kill them at first sight. This caution and threat was repeated several times in a way that gave the boys to understand that they meant all they said, and would just as leave slay them as not if they suspected anything had been revealed by them.

Everything being ready, the boys started off in charge of the guard. Right glad they were to once more gain the open air with so good a prospect for their lives, and they breathed a sigh of relief and satisfaction when they were out of sight of the house in which they had endured such great peril. They took an unfrequented road down toward the Mississippi River which runs around one side of Nauvoo. Some of the guards were very much dissatisfied with the way the tables had turned, and, when they got a safe distance from the house, they halted to consider if it would not be best to slay the boys on their own responsibility. They would glady have murdered them . . . (except for fear of discovery); but, after some discussion, they contented themselves by reiterating the cautions and threats that had been given the boys so many times. They continued their march until within a few rods of the river, when they halted . . . "Well, I guess we have gone about far enough, and had better turn back." Then turning to the boys, he continued, "Boys, if you ever open your mouths concerning anything you have seen or heard in any of our meetings; we will kill you by night or by day wherever we find you, and consider it our duty."

"Oh, don't fear on that account," replied the boys, anxious to allay their uneasiness, lest they still might take a notion to slay them and cast their bodies into the river, "we can see that it is greatly to our advantage . . . to keep silent concerning these things."

"I'm glad you've got sense enough to see it in that light," was the rejoinder in a tone that indicated that his mind was somewhat relieved.

During this conversation, one of the boys looked towards the river, to his great surprise, saw a hand rise into view from behind the bank and beckon for them to come that way. The guards, after admonishing them once more to be silent, and telling them their lives depended upon their keeping the secret, turned to retrace their steps just as one of the boys, anxious to put them at ease, said to his companion: "Let's go down to the river."

"Yes," returned the guard, evidently pleased with that arrangement; "you had better go down to the river."

The reader will readily understand that the meeting had lasted until a late hour in the afternoon and the conspirators had already detained the boys so long that they were afraid their parents and friends, some of whom perhaps knew where the boys had gone, would become anxious and begin to suspect foul play, and possibly might institute a search which would prove exceedingly disadvantageous to the conspiracy. The boys therefore very adroitly proposed to go to the river, so if they were found there it would be sufficient explanation for their long absence. The guards perceived the idea instantly, and it pleased them, for it indicated to them that the boys wished to keep the secret, and avoid being questioned too closely.

The boys started on the run toward the river, but, lest the guards should watch them, and discover the presence of Joseph, whose hand it was they had seen above the bank, they directed their course to a point about a quarter of a mile beyond where Joseph was, knowing he would follow them. On reaching the river, they stepped down the bank and there awaited the arrival of the Prophet, while the guards returned to the meeting. It seems that Joseph, knowing the danger into which the boys had gone, had become so uneasy at their long absence that he could no longer remain at home, so he and one of his body guards, John Scott, who was the brother of Robert, started out to see if they could discover what had become of them. Perhaps they suspected the boys had been murdered and that their bodies would be thrown into the stream, as William Law's house, where the meeting was held, was but a short distance from the river. At all events they were under the bank when the boys were liberated, and now glided around close to the water's edge to the point where the boys were awaiting them.

It was a joyful meeting; Joseph seemed delighted to see that the boys had escaped with their lives. The party walked to a point nearly opposite Joseph's store, where a board fence came down to the edge of the river, forming, together with the orchard trees and shrubbery, a suitable retreat where they could converse without danger of being seen or heard.

"Let us sit down here," said Joseph. All four of them entered the secluded retreat, and when they were seated he continued: "Boys, we saw your danger and were afraid you would not get out alive, but we are thankful that you got off safely. Now relate to me all that you have witnessed."

The boys then gave him a complete account of all they had witnessed and passed through; repeated to him the oath they had seen and heard administered to some two hundred individuals separately; gave him the names of all they knew that had taken the oath; in short they gave him a most accurate recital of all they had seen and heard.

Joseph and his companion listened very attentively, and, as the boys proceeded, a very grave expression crept over the countenance of the former, showing that a deep anxiety was preying upon his mind. When the recital was finished a pause of some length ensued. Joseph was very much moved, and at length burst out: "O, brethren, you do not know what this will terminate in!" But proceeded no further, for his feelings were so strong that he burst into tears. In great agitation Brother John Scott, who was an intimate and trusted friend of Joseph, sprang forward and throwing his arms around the Prophet's neck, exclaimed: "O, Brother Joseph! do you think they are going to kill you?" and they fell on each other's necks and wept bitterly. The scene is difficult to describe. The thought of losing their friend and Prophet by the hands of such a bloodthirsty mob was sufficient to wring their hearts; and those brave men who but a few minutes before had fearlessly faced death, and scorned the proffered conditions on which their lives might be spared, now wept like children and mingled their tears with those of their leader.

Joseph was the first to master his feelings, and, raising Brother Scott's arms from off his neck, he said, in a deep and sorrowful tone: "I fully comprehend it!" He then relaxed into a solemn study, while his brethren watched the changes in his countenance as if they would read the thoughts and feelings that were preying upon his heart. The scene was painful and impressive. Each moment they expected to hear him say that his work on earth was done and that he would have to be slain to seal his testimony. After a long silence he finally continued:

"Brethren, I am going to leave you. I shall not be with you long; it will not be many months until I shall have to go."

This remark still left them in doubt as to his future fate; but it had such significance that Brother Scott again anxiously inquired, "Brother Joseph, are you going to be slain?"

Joseph, for some reason, evaded a direct reply, but continued in a tone that told too plainly of the sorrow he felt: "I am going away and will not be known among this people for twenty years of more. I shall remain a season."

This reply did not clear away their doubts any more than the former one, but it was evident he intended to leave the people and keep hid more closely than he ever had done, or else, with prophetic vision, he discerned the final outcome of his enemies efforts, and, through compassion, forebore to crush the spirits of his brethren by telling them plainly the whole truth.

Subsequent events leave us still in doubt as to the real purport of his words. The dark clouds of persecution from enemies without, fearfully augmented by traitors within, grew so threatening that he saw that something must be done for the safety of himself and the people. He therefore conceived the idea of moving the Saints once more, and this time far beyond the cruel blasts of persecution, and seek a shelter behind the barriers of the Rocky Mountains. He called for a company of volunteers to explore the Great West to find the most suitable place for the Saints to settle. Quite a number volunteered and began to make preparations for the journey. It is a well known fact that just previous to surrendering himself to be taken to Carthage, Joseph got into a boat and started across the river to evade his enemies. He intended to keep out of their hands until this company had procured a suitable outfit for such an undertaking, when he would have accompanied them. Some of his brethren, however, begged him not to desert the people in such a time of trouble and danger, and at their importunity he returned to Nauvoo, and we all know the result. He was induced to surrender himself to the officers of the law, was cast into prison, and there cruelly murdered by a bloodthirsty mob.

Perhaps in his reply to Brother Scott's question Joseph was revolving these plans in his mind and looking forward to the time when he and the Saints would be beyond the reach of persecution; it is now impossible to tell, but the events which followed rather indicate that he foresaw his death. However, he continued with great earnestness.

"They accuse me of polygamy, and of being a false Prophet, and many other things. . . . But I am no false Prophet; I am no imposter; I have had no dark revelations; I have had no revelations from the devil; I made no revelations; I have got nothing up of myself. The same God that has thus far dictated me and directed me and strengthened me in this work, gave me this revelation and commandment on celestial and plural marriage, and the same God commanded me to obey it. He said to me that unless I accepted it and introduced it, and practiced it, I, together with my people, would be damned and cut off from this time henceforth. And they said if I do so, they will kill me! Oh, what shall I do? If I do not practice it, I shall be damned with my people. If I do teach it, and practice it, and urge it, they say they will kill me, and I know they will. But," said he, "we have got to observe it. It is an eternal principle and was given by way of commandment and not by way of instruction."

It will be seen by these outbursts of his soul what a conflict was going on in his mind; and the agony that he endured can only be imagined by those who knew his sensitive and generous spirit. Persecution and imprisonment from the hands of an enemy would be passed by almost unnoticed when compared with these murderous thrusts from the daggers of alienated friends. Death, to a man so familiar with the unseen world and the happiness there, was stripped of its terrors. His fear of simply losing his life caused him little anxiety. But his whole soul was in the work which the Lord had given him to do, and such bloodthirsty opposition to a commandment of God among his brethren caused the greatest anxiety and grief. His greatest trials are no doubt hid deepest from our view.

The consultation lasted for a long time before they separated to their homes, and impressions were made on the minds of our two young heroes that will last forever. They got an insight into the life of the Prophet and the motive of the work he had to perform that had never before entered their imaginations. Their love for him and the cause for which he was laboring was increased, and gladly would they have laid down their lives to have saved his.

Before separating, however, Joseph placed a seal upon the boys' lips, and made them promise that they would not reveal what had transpired that day to a living soul—not even to their own fathers,—for at least twenty years. The object of placing this injuction upon them no doubt was for their own safety, as their lives would probably have been taken if any of the conspirators should ever find that any of their proceedings had been revealed. [6]

The year before Brigham Young died, Den invited him to stay at the Harris family home in Monroe while enroute to St. George. Den then related the foregoing story. President Young said it cleared up many otherwise unanswered questions concerning the plots againt the Prophet.

Young Den was a member of the Nauvoo Legion, as was his older brother Martin H., and therefore both were present at the laying of the corner stone of the Nauvoo Temple on April 6, 1841.

In Nauvoo, Den became acquainted with Margaret Allen, the lovely young daughter of James Dickerson and Sarah Ann Hardy Allen from Salem County, New Jersey. They had gathered with the Saints in Nauvoo to cast their lots with others who had joined the Church in far away places. A friendship developed quickly between Den and Margaret that could have led to a youthful courtship. However, Margaret's parents frowned upon Den's attentions because he was a nephew of Martin Harris, who had through his own folly failed to follow the leadership of Joseph Smith and therefore had remained in Kirtland, Ohio.[7] Little did they then know that their paths would cross again in years yet to come.

Words cannot describe this young man's feelings as word came of the death of his dear friend and beloved prophet, Joseph Smith, Jr. After partially recovering from the grief and shock, all faithful Saints put forth every effort to carry on to complete the unfinished Nauvoo Temple and to exhibit their loyalty to their new leader, Brigham Young. Dennison was blessed to perform sacred ordinances for himself in the Nauvoo Temple on February 7, 1846.[8]

In the fall of 1846, Den went on a scouting expedition. He left home in September three days before the Battle of Nauvoo, and journeyed several hundred miles westward, exploring the way for the exodus of the Saints. He then returned to help his father, Emer, and his own family leave the deserted city, eventually arriving in Kanesville, Iowa.

In Council Bluffs, on March 7, 1847, Dennison married Sarah Wilson Cheney, a young widow with one child, Mary Ellender, whom he later adopted as his own. Their marriage was sealed by Brigham Young at Winter Quarters, Iowa, on March 31, 1848.[9]

Den remained in Pottawattamie County until 1852. It appears that he and his father, Emer, had been requested by Church leaders to remain at this outpost to assist pioners preparing to cross the plains, by making and repairing wagons for the poor emigrants. Emer was an experienced carpenter and Den a blacksmith; Charles, a younger brother, became the errand boy. Other members of the Harris family had gone west in 1850. As the 27th Quorum of Seventies met in Great Salt Lake City on December 4, 1851, Thomas Bullock reported that Dennison Lott Harris and a few other members of the quorum were still in Iowa.[10]

By 1852, when they joined Emer and Charles to emigrate to Utah, Den and Sarah had two additional daughters, Deborah Jane and Sarah Ann.

They arrived at their destination in October, 1852, with Captain Cutler's Company. Here they joined other members of the Harris family now settled in northern Utah. But Den left his wife and children three more times to help other emigrants cross the western plains.

The first ten years after their arrival, Den and his growing family lived in several different settlements in Utah: Springville, Alpine, Smithfield, and Willard. During this time three sons were born to Den and Sarah: Dennison Emer, Martin, and Hyrum.

In Springville, in about 1854, President Young called sixteen men, including Dennison L. Harris, William and Dimick B. Huntington, Lot Smith, Levi G. Metcalf, to go on a mission to the Navajo Indians. There were also two interpreters and an Indian guide called Highford (meaning "high forehead"). President Young accompanied them as far as Manti, where he blessed them, promising them that if they would keep the commandments of the Lord, not a hair of their heads would be harmed, and they would return to their families in safety.

In Salina canyon they wre delayed by a band of Indians who refused to let them cross the stream of water on penalty of death. Three days later, the Indians relented. Further on, they discovered coal at a site they named Huntington for members of their group.

In the area of the Green River, Utah, the Indians again tried to stop them. The missionaries turned into a cottonwood cove where they were completely hidden. They cached their wagons and some supplies and continued their journey on horseback.

Near a place now called Bluff, they were taken prisoners by the Navajos. Two of the party were to be shot. Sixteen Indians stood poised with bows and arrows, but at the signal, all sixteen Indians were paralyzed, unable to commit the wicked deed. The missionaries were then allowed to preach the gospel to the tribe, but they were still looked upon with suspicion by all except the chief, who never left them for a moment. The Indian council finally decreed that the strangers were to be killed on a given day, chief or no chief.

The day was drawing near when a terrible war-whoop and clouds of dust filled the air. The Navajos were completely surrounded by the Elk Mountain Utes. Their chief pointed a gun at the Navajo chief. An uproar followed. Finally the interpreters quieted the tribes, and the Ute chief explained that the Great Spirit had appeared to him and told him the Navajos had white men in captivity. He had been commanded to release the white men and their property, to accompany them several day's journey on a certain route, and then outfit them with good horses and provisions. If he failed, destruction would fall upon his own tribe. The Navajos were sufficiently impressed. They released the missionaries to the care of the Utes, who fulfilled the commission to the letter.

The return of the missionaries was along a different route, so they missed their cached wagons. Provisions grew very low. One man, Metcalf, lost his horse. Den Harris remained with him to hunt for it. This put them one day behind the main company, who themselves faced starvation. Each day two biscuits were placed upon sticks for Den and his companion. When they didn't catch up with the main party, they were given up for dead. The company returned through Hobble Creek Canyon, having run out of bread the previous day. The people of Springville went out to meet the returning missionaries with wagons and food, but the men were so ill and weak they had to take simple nourishment at short intervals. But every man returned to his family, as he had been promised, and each regained his health and strength. [11]

It was while the family was living in Alpine, Utah, that Father Emer, while visiting there, gave both Den and Sarah their patriarchal blessings, dated August 12, 1855.

> My son, Dennison L. Harris, I lay my hands upon your head . . . and [give you] a father's blessing . . . because of thy integrity and thy faith for embracing the everlasting gospel in the days of thy childhood and have [having] remained faithful until the present . . . a multiplicity of blessings shall be poured out upon you and thou shalt go from strength to strength until thou shalt became a mighty man in the hands of God. . . . Fear not, my son, but be strong in the Lord and not a hair of thy head shall fall by an enemy.[12]

One of Dennison's children, Martin L., reported that during one of their moves they stopped in Salt Lake City, where for the first time they tasted peaches, and candy made of sugar.

In 1862 Den decided to go to Dixie (southern Utah), where his brother, Charles, had recently moved his family. Den went particularly for his father's failing health. They settled first at Bellevue and later at Virgin City, where their youngest son, Joseph Alma, was born.

Den's health began to fail under the rigors of pioneer life. He suffered from chills and fevers. About 1868

> he was so ill that those waiting upon him came into the room where the family was, and told them that their husband and father was dead. Kindly neighbors went into the death chamber to prepare the body for burial. The body quivered and Brother Harris opened his eyes. He told family and friends that his spirit had left his body. The male guide; who was with him had said, "Brother Harris, all is well with you. Your salvation is assured; but if you wish, you may return to earth, raise your boys and enter into Celestial [plural] marriage."[13]

He made the choice to return to life and did later receive these blessings.

*Home of Dennison Lott Harris at Virgin City, Utah.
Built between 1863-1865.*

In 1872 the family moved to Monroe, Utah, where they established a family home. Den started the first nursery in that region and gave away hundreds of trees and shrubs to friends and neighbors to help them beautify their home surroundings.

Though the Harris family moved often, each move bettered their conditions. To Monroe, they brought cows, horses, sheep, pigs, chickens, farm implements, and household goods. Almost as soon as they arrived, Den and sons broke up eighty acres of land and planted it. Their home was always open to weary travelers who found food and lodging for themselves and their animals. Sarah was a gracious hostess who, along with her husband, shared freely with others.

But the close companionship of Den and Sarah came to a close with the passing of Sarah on February 23, 1875. The obituary, published in the Deseret News two months later, April 21, 1875, tells all too briefly of her noble life:

> At Monroe, Sevier Co., Feb. 23, SARAH wife of Dennison L. Harris and daughter of James and Eleanor Wilson.
>
> Deceased was born at Shelbyville, Bedford County, Tennessee, Sept. 20, 1824; baptized near Adam-ondi-Ahman when about thirteen years of age; suffered cruel hardships with the Saints in their expulsion from Missouri; gathered with the Saints to these valleys in 1852; was a great sufferer at intervals, for the past ten years, from dyspepsia, agravated (sic) by her trying age, and finally dropped asleep as calmy as an infant in its mother's arms, without a pang She was a most exemplary wife and mother, and very highly esteemed by an extensive and numerous circle of friends. She left a husband and six children.[14]

Not long afterward, the United Order was established. Except for what Den needed for the care of his own family, he turned everything over to the Order. Because of poor management, poverty, and perhaps some selfishness on the part of the members of the Order, it failed. It was formally dissolved byErastus Snow, who chose Dennison Lott Harris to serve as the bishop of the Monroe Ward on July 17, 1877.

Bishop Harris chose as his counselors two men who represented the opposing factions of the Order. He hoped by this to once again unite the people. At the first meeting, after the reorganization of the bishopric, Den pled with the people to bury the past and to work together in love and cooperation, a goal which was eventually accomplished.

Nine years after Sarah's death, Dennison Lott Harris married plural wives in the St. George Temple, on November 1, 1883. One was Anna Maria Messerli, a young Swiss convert. The other, a widow, Margaret Allen, was his childhood sweetheart from long-ago Nauvoo days.

Margaret Allen had married in the Endowment House, May 14, 1852, Charles Young Webb, by whom she had five children. Later, she had married John Glover Smith, by whom she had three children.[15] Yet in her later life, she chose to be sealed for eternity to Dennison Lott Harris.

Den served the people of Monroe as their bishop until his death from pneumonia, which occurred June 6, 1885, at Monroe, Utah. But fate had not allowed him to see the little daughter born to him and Anna Maria. The child, Harriet Lott (known as Lottie), came into the world a few days after her father's burial. She was born June 13, 1885.[16]

Den's obituary was as follows:

> The funeral services were held in the new meeting house, which was draped in mourning for the occasion. About one thousand people assembled to pay their respects to the departed. The speakers all bore testimony of his excellent qualities, his true integrity to the cause of God and his brethren, his unwavering faith, his readiness at all times to give counsel, his many fatherly traits of character, and the honorable and loving family left to perpetuate his name.

Fifty three vehicles followed his remains to the grave.[17]

Dennison Lott Harris is buried in the Monroe Cemetery, where a suitable monument honors him and his wives.

FOOTNOTES

Dennison Lott Harris

[1]"Family Record of Emer Harris," March 19, 1868, in a family publication, *Martin Henderson Harris – A Utah Pioneer*, July 21, 1952, p.1; hereafter cited as M.H.H.

[2]Franklin S. Harris, Sr., MSS 340, in Special Collections, Harold B. Lee Library, Brigham Young University, Provo, Utah; hereafter cited as "Writing of Emer Harris."

[3]Ibid.

[4]Lottie Harris Hayes, private letters and papers in possession of Belle H. Wilson.

[5]Ibid.

[6]Horace H. Cummings, "The Conspiracy of Nauvoo", *The Contributor*, vol. V, 1884.

[7]Allen family oral tradition.

[8]Nauvoo Temple Records, alphabetical index, Genealogical Department of the Church of Jesus Christ of Latter-day Saints.

[9]Special Collection, March 31, 1848, Genealogical Department.

[10]*Journal History*, December 4, 1851, Historical Department, The Church of Jesus Christ of Latter-day Saints.

[11]Hayes, private letters and papers.

[12]Emer Harris to Dennison Lott Harris, Patriarchal Blessing, August 12, 1855, Vol. 210, #308, Historical Department, p.91.

[13]Hayes, private letters and papers.

[14]"Obituary", *Deseret News*, Apr. 21, 1875, p.179.

[15]Patrons Record, under surnames of husbands, Genealogical Archives, Genealogical Department.

[16]Harris family genealogy records in possession of Belle H. Wilson.

[17]William A. Warnock, "Obituary of Dennison Lott Harris", in possession of Belle H. Wilson.

The authors wish to acknowledge the help of Franklin S. Harris, Jr., for supplying pictures, private family notes, letters, papers, and so forth, including the writing of Lottie Harris Hayes (deceased).

BIBLIOGRAPHY

Dennison Lott Harris

PUBLISHED MATERIALS

Contributor, vol. V, 1884.

Deseret News. Salt Lake City, 1875.

Family Record of Emer Harris, in family publication, *Martin Henderson Harris — A Utah Pioneer*, 1952.

Harris, Franklin S. Sr. In Special Collections, Harold B. Lee Library, Brigham Young University, Provo, Utah.

Journal History, 11877, in collection of The Church of Jesus Christ of Latter-day Saints, Historical Department.

UNPUBLISHED MATERIALS

Allen family oral tradition.

Harris, Emer to Dennison Lott Harris. Patriarchal Blessing, vol. 210. In collection of The Church of Jesus Christ of Latter-day Saints, Historical Department.

Harris family genealogy records in possession of Belle H. Wilson.

Hayes, Lottie Harris. Private letters and papers in possession of Belle H. Wilson.

Nauvoo Temple Records. In collection of The Church of Jesus Christ of Latter-day Saints, Genealogical Department.

Patrons Record. In collection of The Church of Jesus Christ of Latter-day Saints, Genealogical Archives.

Special Collection, 1848. In collection of The Church of Jesus Christ of Latter-day Saints, Genealogical Department.

VIII.
Harris Family Genealogy

PEDIGREE CHART

NATHAN HARRIS FAMILY

Submitted by Co-authors Belle H. Wilson, Madge H. Tuckett

CHART NO. _____

STREET ADDRESS _____

CITY _____ STATE _____

NO. 1 ON THIS CHART IS
THE SAME PERSON AS NO. _____

ON CHART NO. _____

1. Emer HARRIS
   Martin "
   Preserved "
   Solomon "
   Seville "
   Sophia "
   Lydia "
   Naomi "

2a. Rufus HARRIS
2. Nathan HARRIS
BORN 23 Mar 1758
WHERE Smithfield, Prov. R.I.
WHEN MARRIED
DIED 17 Nov 1835
WHERE Mentor, Lake, Ohio

3. Rhoda LAPHAM
BORN 27 Apr 1759
WHERE Providence, Prov. R.I.
DIED 11 Oct 1849
WHERE Mentor, Lake, Ohio

4. Preserved HARRIS
BORN 15 June 1715
WHERE Providence, Prov. R.I.
WHEN MARRIED 26 Apr 1744
DIED 6 May 1797
WHERE Smithfield, Prov. R.I.

5. Martha MOWRY
BORN 1 Apr 1726
WERE Smithfield, Prov. R.I.
DIED
WHERE

6. Solomon LAPHAM
BORN 1 Aug 1730
WHERE Dartmouth, Bristol, Mass.
WHEN MARRIED 28 Feb 1756
DIED 1800
WHERE Glocester, Prov. R.I.

7. Sylvia LAPHAM
BORN 8 May 1731
WHERE Smithfield, Prov. R.I.
DIED May 1805
WHERE Glocester, Prov. R.I.

8. Richard HARRIS
BORN 14 Oct 1668
WHERE Providence, Prov. R.I.
WHEN MARRIED
DIED 18 Aug 1750
WHERE Smithfield, Prov. R.I.

9. Elizabeth KING
BORN abt 1680
WHERE Marshfield, Plymouth, Mass.
DIED 28 Mar 1736 age 56
WHERE Provide: :e, Prov. R.I.

10. Uriah MOWRY
BORN 15 Aug 1705
WHERE Smithfield, Prov. R.I.
WHEN MARRIED
DIED 6 Mar 1792
WHERE

11. Urania PAINE
BORN 4 July 1706
WHERE Rehobath, Bristol, Mass.
DIED 4 Mar 1772
WHERE

12. Nicholas LAPHAM
BORN 1 Apr 1689
WHERE Dartmouth, Bristol, Mass.
DIED 1 Dec 1726
WHERE

13. Mercy ARNOLD
BORN 22 Dec 1701
WHERE Providence, Prov. R.I.
DIED
WHERE Dartmouth, Bristol, Mass

14. Thomas LAPHAM
BORN 10 Dec 1705
WHERE Dartmouth, Bristol, Mass.
WHEN MARRIED 4 Feb 1729/30
DIED 5 Jan 1779
WHERE Smithfield, Prov. R.I.

15. Abigail WILBUR
BORN 9 Sept 1711
WHERE Portsmouth, Newport, R.I.
DIED
WHERE

16. Thomas HARRIS
   ABOVE NAME CONTINUED ON CHART

17. Elnathan TEW
   ABOVE NAME CONTINUED ON CHART

18. Clement KING
   ABOVE NAME CONTINUED ON CHART

9. Elizabeth BAKER
   ABOVE NAME CONTINUED ON CHART

20. Henry MOWRY
   ABOVE NAME CONTINUED ON CHART

21. Mary BULL
   ABOVE NAME CONTINUED ON CHART

22. John PAINE
   ABOVE NAME CONTINUED ON CHART

23. Elizabeth BELCHER
   ABOVE NAME CONTINUED ON CHART

24. John LAPHAM
   ABOVE NAME CONTINUED ON CHART

25. Mary MANN
   ABOVE NAME CONTINUED ON CHART

26. John ARNOLD
   ABOVE NAME CONTINUED ON CHART

27. Mary MOWRY
   ABOVE NAME CONTINUED ON CHART

28. John LAPHAM
   ABOVE NAME CONTINUED ON CHART

29. Mary RUSSELL
   ABOVE NAME CONTINUED ON CHART

30. Benjamin WILBORE
   ABOVE NAME CONTINUED ON CHART

31. Elizabeth HEAD
   ABOVE NAME CONTINUED ON CHART

NAME OF RECORDS WHERE THIS INFORMATION WAS OBTAINED:

Archive Records
Family Records
Temple Records
Early Records of R.I. and Mass.

LITHOGRAPHED IN U.S.A.
COPYRIGHTED, 1938 GENEALOGICAL SOCIETY OF UTAH

The following pages of genealogical information will provide data with which hundreds may connect their four-generation research into these lines of descent.

Providence, R.I. Oath of Allegiance, Preamble:

"I do declare and Promife That I will be true and ffaithfull to the comonwealth of England, as it is now Establifhed, without a king or houfe of Lords." Signed by twelve men, eight of whom later signed to be loyal to King Charles II. The Oath was originally signed in the 1650's when Oliver Cromwell ruled England, then again signed in 1666-67 with a declaration of loyalty to a king.

Providence, Rhode Island, was settled sixteen years after the Plymouth Colony and six years after the Colony of the Massachusetts Bay. No other town of as early an origin has so many town records. This is remarkable when it is remembered that the town was destroyed in the King Phillip's War. John Smith Jr., the miller, was town clerk from 1672-1676. When the Indians set fire to his house and the Town Records were likely to be burned, Smith threw the records into the mill pond. They were later recovered and taken to Newport. Roger Williams, in noting their return from Newport in April the following year, says that they were "saved by God's merciful Providence from fire and water."

At the time of the signing of the Oath, Roger Williams was in England endeavoring to persuade Parliament to restore the charter of 1643.

Roger Williams (b. abt. 1599, d. 1683) embarked for the colonies from England December 1, 1630 in the ship "Lyon." On the ship were Thomas and William Harris, Thomas Angell and others. They arrived in Salem, Mass., February 1631. Williams and Harris were banished from Massachusetts for liberal religious views. They spent the winter with the Indians, then settled Mooshausick, later called Providence.

HARRIS FAMILY GENEALOGY

(see printed pedigree)

Thomas and Elizabeth (Leatherland) Harris immigrated from England in 1630 on the ship *Lyon*. Parents of six children. Settled in Rhode Island.

16. Thomas and Elnathan (Tew) Harris. Parents of nine children. Rhode Island.

8. Richard and Elizabeth (King) Harris. Parents of nine children. Rhode Island.

4. Preserved and Martha (Mowry) Harris. Rhode Island. Parents of nine children, including sons Rufus and Nathan Harris.

2a. Rufus Harris
    b.   23 Nov 1749, Smithfield, Prov., R.I.
    md. Lucy (Hill?), b. abt 1750, R.I.
    d.   30 May 1798, Palmyra, Ontario, N.Y.

Children born in Smithfield, R.I.:
I. Paul Harris
      b.   8 May 1774
      md. name unknown. Several children
      d.   1821
II. Martha Harris
      b.   5 Jan 1776, Smithfield
      md. Adam Hills
      d.   ?
III. Peter Harris
      b.   23 Apr 1778
      md. Abigail ————
      d.   7 Apr 1849
      A Quaker minister
IV. Levi Harris
      b.   6 July 1781
      md. Remember ————
      d.   27 Mar 1859

V. Martin P. Harris
   b.   15 June 1782
   md. Elizabeth ———————
   d.   1826
VI. Arthur Harris
   b.   11 Sept 1785
   md. name unknown. Several children
   d.   25 Jan 1811
VIII. Seth Harris
   b.   11 Feb 1788
   md. Sophia Harris (his cousin)
   d.   19 Dec 1821 by drowning
VIII. Betsy Harris
   b.   8 Apr 1790, probably at Palmyra, N.Y.
   md. ———————Midbury
   d.   ?
IX. Lucy Harris
   b.   1 May 1792, probably Palmyra, N.Y.
   md. 27 Mar 1808, Martin Harris (her cousin)
   d.   1836 at Palmyra, N.Y.
X. Polly (Mary) Harris
   b.   8 Mar 1794, probably Palmyra, N.Y.
   md. (1) 3 Jan 1812, Freeman Cobb. He drowned
         19 Dec 1821. Several children
   md. (2) 3 July 1828, William Parker. Several chil-
         dren
   d.   18 Dec 1871

Sources of information:
Vital Records of Smithfield, Prov., R.I.
Will of Peter Harris #3 in Surrogate Court, Lyons, Wayne, N.Y.
Fate of "Atlas Schooner," Dec 1821, published in *The Ontario Times.*
Additions welcomed.

2. Nathan Harris
    b. 23 Mar 1758, Smithfield, Prov., R.I.
    md. Rhoda Lapham. See pedigree for information
    d. 17 Nov 1835, Mentor, Lake, Ohio.
    Children:
    I. Emer Harris
        b. 29 May 1781, Cambridge, Wash., N.Y.
        md. Several times - see his record
        d. 28 Nov 1869, Logan, Cache, Utah
    II. Martin Harris
        b. 18 May 1783, Easton, Saratoga, N.Y.
        md. twice - see his record
        d. 10 July 1875, Clarkston, Cache, Utah
    III. Preserved Harris
        b. 8 May 1785, Easton, Saratoga, N.Y.
        md. Nancy Warren. Several children
        d. 18 Apr 1867
    IV. Solomon Harris
        b. 18 Mar 1787, Easton, Saratoga, N.Y.
        md. Elmira ————
        d. 11 Oct 1828
    V. Seville Harris
        b. abt 1790, Easton, Saratoga, N.Y.
    VI. Sophia Harris
        b. abt 1792, Easton, Saratoga, N.Y.
        md. 25 May 1806, Seth Harris (a cousin)
    VII. Lydia Harris
        b. abt 1793, Probably Palmyra, Ontario, N.Y.
        md. Nathaniel Davenport
    VIII. Naomi Harris
        b. 5 May 1795, Palmyra, N.Y.
        md. (1) Benjamin Deuel. One child

        md. (2) 12 Oct 1826, Ezekiel Kellogg. Three chil-
               dren
        md. (3) after 1865, Samuel Bent (no issue)
            d. 29 Mar 1884

MARTIN HARRIS FAMILY

1. Martin Harris
    b. 18 May 1783, Easton, Wash. (now Saratoga), N.Y.
    md. (1) 27 Mar 1808, Lucy Harris (a cousin) at Palmyra, Ontario (now Wayne), N.Y.
    d. 10 July 1875, Clarkston, Cache, Utah
    Children:
    I. Lucy Harris
        b. abt 1809, Palmyra, N.Y.
        md. 8 May 1828, Flanders, Dyke, N.Y.
        d. 1841
    II. Duty Harris
        b. abt 1811, Palmyra, N.Y.
        d. 1815
    III. George B. Harris
        b. 1813 - age 37 yrs in 1850 census
        md. (1) Mary A————. Three children
        md. (2) 28 Dec 1858, Mary J.Thompson in Kirtland, Ohio. Child, Alma Harris
        d. 1864 after a medical discharge for illness during the Civil War.
    IV. Elizabeth (Betsy) Harris
        b. 1821 - age 29 yrs in 1850 census
        md. 17 Feb 1837, Amos Adams. Three daughters
        d. 23 July 1855 in Henry Co., Iowa
    Probably other children such as:
    ? Henry M. Harris
        b. 1810 - age 40 in 1850 census of Calhoun Co., Mich.
        md. Ellinor ————. Eight children
        d. before 1860 census

Sources of information:
Census Records of Palmyra, N.Y. and Kirtland, Ohio, 1850, 1860, 1870; of Calhoun Co. Mich 1850 for child #3 and Henry.
Will of Peter Harris
George's application for Civil War Pension
George's marriage record in Kirtland, Ohio

After the death of Martin's wife Lucy Harris, the summer of 1836 Martin married:

(2) 1 Nov 1836, Caroline Young
    b.   17 May 1816 at Hectar, Schuyler, N.Y., the daughter of John and Theodocia (Kimball) Young

Children:

I. Martin Harris Jr.
    b.   28 Jan 1838 at Kirtland, Geauga, Ohio
    md. (1) 1 Nov 1859, Nancy Ann Homer
  md (2) 8 June 1867, Mary Imagene Corbett
  md (3) 22 Oct 1879, Mary Ann Morton
    d.   27 Sept 1913

II. Daughter
    b.   abt 1839
    d.   between 1840-1850

III. Julia Lacothia
    b.   29 Apr 1842, Kirtland, Lake, Ohio
    md. 1 Mar 1860, Elijah W. Davis
    d.   6 Feb 1869

IV. John Wheeler Harris
    b.   11 July 1845, Kirtland, Ohio
    md. 12 Dec 1870, Emily Amelia Brimm
    d.   Aug 1916

V. Sarah Harris
    b.   1849 - age 1 yr in 1850 Census of Kirtland, Ohio
    d.   before 1860 census

VI. Solomon Webster Harris
    b.   1 Dec 1854, Kirtland, Ohio
    md. 24 Dec 1874, Maryetta Rice
    d.   3 Mar 1919

VII. Ida May Harris
    b.   27 May 1856 in Iowa
    md. (1) 1872, Allan Findley Crockett
    md. (2) abt 1884, Alma Harris (a relative)

Caroline (Young) Harris:

> md. (2) 16 Jan 1860, John Catley Davis by whom she
>   had one child:
>
> I. Joseph Harris Davis
>   b.   19 Nov 1860, Payon, Utah, Utah
>   d.   21 Nov 1860, Payon, Utah, Utah
>   Caroline died 17 Jan 1888 at Lewisville, Bingham,
>   Idaho.

Sources of information:
Family Records, letters, etc.
Temple Records of Nauvoo and Logan
Early Church records
Martin Harris' Application for Pension from War of 1812
gives his marriage dates.

EMER HARRIS FAMILY

1. Emer - sons of Nathan and Rhoda (Lapham) Harris
   b. 29 May 1781, Cambridge, Wash., N.Y.
   md. (1) 22 July 1802, Roxanna Peas
       Divorced 1819, Luzerne Co., Pa.
       Six children born in Palmyra, N.Y.:
   I. Selina Harris
      b. 10 Oct 1803
      d. 19 Feb 1814
   II. Elathan Harris
      b. 7 Oct 1805
      md. Northrop Sweet (unknown issue)
   III. Alvira Harris
      b. 7 Aug 1807
      md. Feb 1829, Benjamin Mosier. Several children
      d. Oct 1891
   IV. Sephrona Harris
      b. 17 Aug 1809
      md. John Manchester. Large family
      d. 19 May 1880
   V. Nathan Harris
      b. 26 Sept 1811
      md. 16 May 1835, Julia Follett (unknown issue)
      d. 14 Feb 1838
   VI. Ruth Harris
      b. 7 Sept 1813
      d. 13 Feb 1829 (unmd)

The above information was taken from the original record of Emer Harris. Additions or corrections would be appreciated by:

Belle H. Wilson   Madge H. Tuckett
273 North 300 East   or   818 North 100 East
American Fork, Utah 84003   American Fork, Utah 84003

Emer married:

(2) 16 Jan 1819, Deborah Lott

b.   Nov or 5 Dec 1799, the daughter of Zephaniah and Rachel (Brown) Lott of Luzerne Co., Pa. Deborah died 6 Mar 1825. Children:

I. Emer Harris

    b.   Nov 1819, Mehoopany, Luzerne, Pa.

    d.   Nov 1819

II. Martin Henderson Harris

    b.   29 Sept 1829, Windham, Luzerne, Pa.

    md. (1) 18 Jan 1855, Georgianna Maria Aldous. One son. Georgianna died

    md. (2) 3 Apr 1859, Louisa Sargent. Had large family.

Pioneer of 1850. Ordained "Seventy" in 1852 in Ogden, Utah.

Founded town of Harrisville in Weber County, Utah

Town's first school teacher.

1876 planted 100 trees in commemoration of anniversary of U.S. Independence.

Served a mission in East.

Loyal husband and father.

Died February 14, 1889 at Harrisville.

III. Harriet Fox Harris

    b.   26 Dec 1822, Windham, Pa.

    md. Moses Judson Daley in Nauvoo, Ill. Came to Utah about 1860, settled in Springville, Utah. Parents of four children

    d.   30 Dec 1810

IV Dennison Lott Harris

    b.   17 Jan 1825, Windham, Pa.

    md. (1) 7 Mar 1847, Sarah (Wilson) Cheney (a widow with one daughter, Mary Ellender Cheney). Sarah and Dennison had six children.

    Sarah died (see obituary).

md. (2) 1 Nov 1883, Anna Maria Messerli, b. 24 Mar 1858, Switzerland, the daughter of Jacob and Magdalena (Sigrist) Messerli. One child, Harriet Lott (Lottie) Harris, b. 13 June 1885; adopted child: Anton M. Harris, b. 13 Nov 1879, Switzerland. Anna M. Harris d. 16 Oct 1889, Monroe, Utah

md. (3) 1 Nov 1883, Margaret Allen (widow Smith)

Dennison d. 6 June 1885 (see obituary).

Emer married:

(3) 29 Mar 1826, Parna Chapell
b. 12 Nov 1792, the daughter of Isaac and Tamison (Wilcox) Chapell, of Mass. and Penn. Parna died 4 June 1857 in Ogden, Weber, Utah. Parents of four children:

I. Fannie Melvina Harris
   b. 21 Jan 1827, Luzerne Co., Pa.
   d. 7 Dec 1841, Nauvoo, Ill
II. Joseph Mormon Harris
   b. 19 July 1830, Mehoopany, Luzerne, Pa.
      Baptized by the Prophet Joseph Smith.
      Came to Utah 1850.
      Crossed the plains twice more to help others.
      Pioneer of Ogden, Utah.
      Had first lumber mill and grist mill there.

   md. 18 Feb 1855, Mary Ann Pons. Parents of ten children
   d. 1 May 1909
III. Alma Harris
   b. 6 June 1832, Brownhelm, Lorain, Ohio
      Came to Utah in 1850.
      Pioneered in Ogden and Logan, Utah
      Involved in the Indian Wars.

Well known as a musician.
Leader of the Military Band.
Played the violin.
First Bishop of the Benson Ward.

md. 15 Mar 1854, Sarah Earl. Parents of nine children

d. 10 Aug 1900

IV. Charles Harris

b. 2 July.1834, Brownhelm, Lorain, Ohio. Came to Utah 1852

md. (1) 20 Apr 1855, Louisa Maria Hall. Parents of eleven children

md. (2) 10 April 1889, Elizabeth Ann Anderson. Parents of four children.
Pioneer of Willard, Box Elder Co., Utah.
Assigned to burn houses, if necessary, at approach of Johnston's Army.
Pioneer in Southern Utah.
Family home in Junction, Piute Co., Utah

d. 3 Feb 1916 in Junction, Utah

Emer married:
(4) 1845 in Nauvoo, Ill., Polly Chamberlain

b. 6 Feb 1812, the daughter of Solomon and Hopestill (Haskins) Chamberlain of Mass. and Ill.

d. between 11 Jan 1848 and 9 June 1849 in Winter Quarters, Nebraska. One child:

I. Rebecca Harris

b. 24 Dec 1845, Nauvoo, Hancock, Ill.
Left motherless at age four.
Came to Utah with relatives in 1850.
Lived in Provo, Utah.

md. (1) 24 Nov 1860, William Joseph Taylor. Had two children. He died.

md. (2) 22 Jan 1871, Hans Peter Peterson. One child raised by his father (after divorce).

md. (3) in 1873, Frank Adams. One child died
young. Divorced.

md. (4) Absolam Yates. Had four children.
Rebecca spent latter part of her life in Lake
Point, Tooele, Utah, where she was presi-
dent of the Relief Society twenty-five years.
Midwife in delivery of many babies.

d.   22 Jan 1929

Emer married:
(5)   10 Sept 1855, Martha Allen

Harris records taken from early L.D.S. Church records
Temple Records
Census Records
Original Journal of Emer Harris
Family Records, private letters, etc.

The following individuals share a common ancestory with Martin Harris:

Franklin S. Harris, Sr. (deceased) Former President of Utah State University
Former President of Brigham Young University
Government assignments to Russia and Japan

Franklin S. Harris, Jr.
Former Professor of Physics, University of Utah
Consultant for Aerospace Corporation, El Segundo, California
Currently researcher on aerosols for Swiss Government

Dallin Harris Oaks
Former President of Brigham Young University
Author of several books
1981, appointed member of Utah Supreme Court

Other descendants of prominence:

Isabell Harris (deceased)
First woman to be imprisoned in Utah Territory as she defended her right to privacy in regard to polygamy.

Sterling H. Nelson
Former member of the General Church Welfare Committee of The Church of Jesus Christ of Latter-day Saints.

Stella H. Oaks (deceased)
Former Utah educator and lecturer

Merril C. Oaks, M.D.
Noted Utah ophthalmologist

Many others who share a common blood line have prominent careers in Utah and other Western localities in the Church, state, and nation.